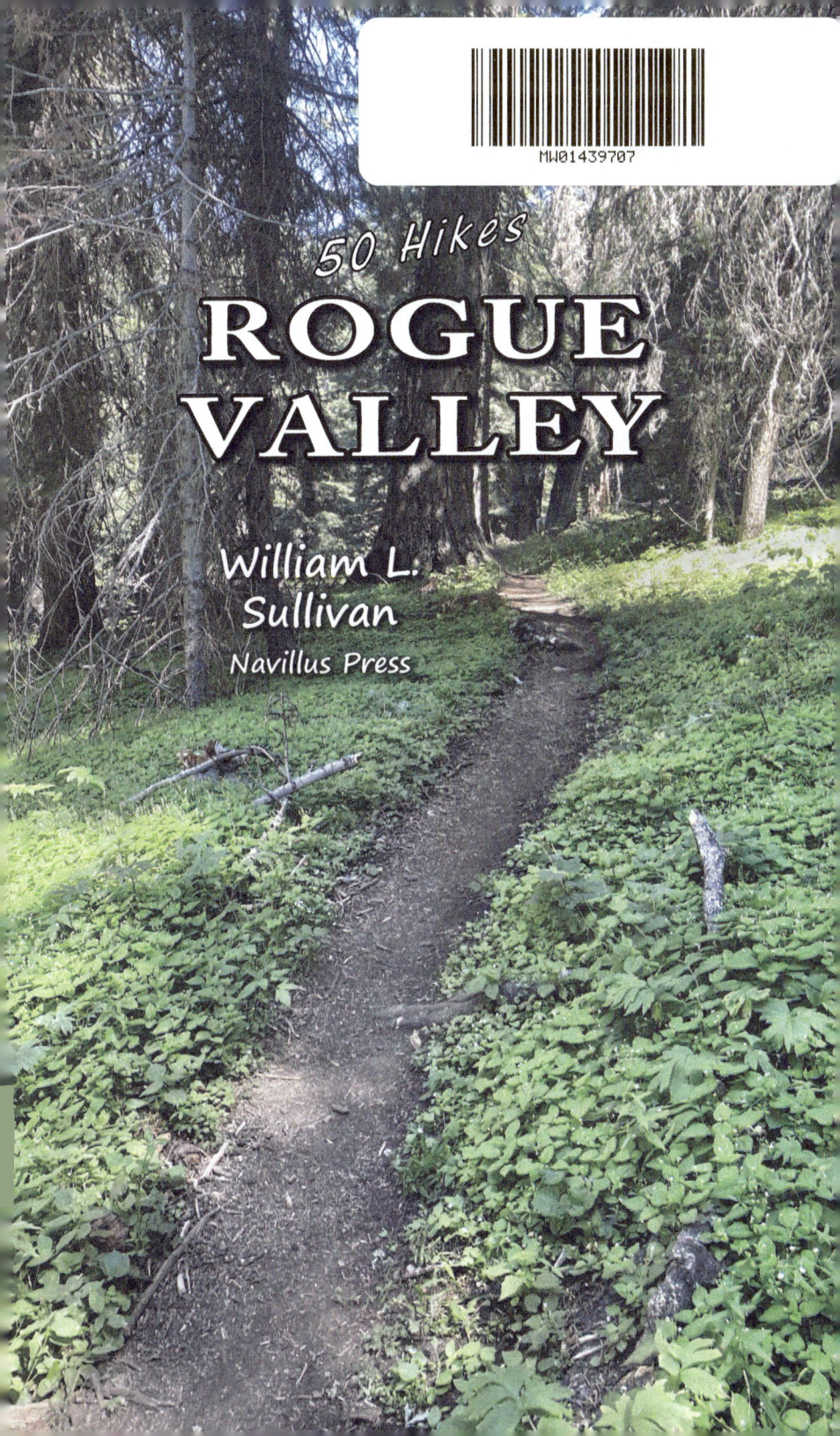

50 Hikes
ROGUE VALLEY

William L. Sullivan

Navillus Press

©2025 by William L. Sullivan
Maps and photography by the author.
All rights reserved. No part of this book
may be reproduced in any form without
written permission from the publisher.

Published by the Navillus Press
1958 Onyx Street
Eugene, Oregon 97403

OregonHiking.com
Printed in USA

Cover: Lilypad Lake and Mt. Shasta from Red Buttes (Hike #20). Back cover: Crater Lake from Rim Village (Hike #37). Frontispiece: The Pacific Crest Trail at Soda Mountain (Hike #4). This page: Crater Lake in winter.

SAFETY CONSIDERATIONS: Many of the trails in this book pass through Wilderness and remote country where hikers are exposed to unavoidable risks. On any hike, the weather may change suddenly. The fact that a hike is included in this book, or that it may be rated as easy, does not necessarily mean it will be safe or easy for you. Prepare yourself with proper equipment and outdoor skills, and you will be able to enjoy these hikes with confidence.
Every effort has been made to assure the accuracy of the information in this book. The author has hiked all of the featured trails. Nonetheless, construction, logging, and storm damage may cause changes. Corrections and updates are welcome, and often rewarded. They may be sent to the publisher, or to *sullivan@efn.org*.

Contents

Highlights of the ROGUE VALLEY
A Visit to Crater Lake 7
A Visit to Oregon Caves 14
Wildlife of Southern Oregon 20
Wildflower Guide 21
Introduction to the Hikes 25

MEDFORD AREA 29
1. Table Rocks 30
2. Roxy Ann Peak 32
3. Grizzly Peak 34
4. Soda Mountain 36
5. Pilot Rock 38
6. Lithia Park 40
7. Bandersnatch Trail 42
8. White Rabbit Trail 44
9. Mount Ashland Meadows 46
10. Split Rock 48
11. Wagner Butte 50
12. Jack-Ash Trail 52
13. East Applegate Ridge 54
14. Sterling Ditch Tunnel 56
15. Jacksonville 58

GRANTS PASS AREA 60
16. Grants Pass Nature Trails 61
17. Enchanted Forest 63
18. Tallowbox Mountain 64
19. Collings Mountain** 66
20. Red Buttes 68
21. Grayback Mountain 70
22. Oregon Caves 72
23. Mount Elijah 74
24. Eight Dollar Mountain 76
25. Illinois River Beaches 78
26. Rogue River Trail East 80
27. Rogue River Trail West 82

Easy / Moderate / Difficult
Great for kids / Open all year / Backpackable

- Horses OK   - Bicycles OK   - Dogs on leash   - No pets
- Wildflowers (count petals for peak month)   *NW Forest Pass site   **Other parking fee
C - Crowded or restricted backpacking area   - Pacific Crest Trail   - Rough access road

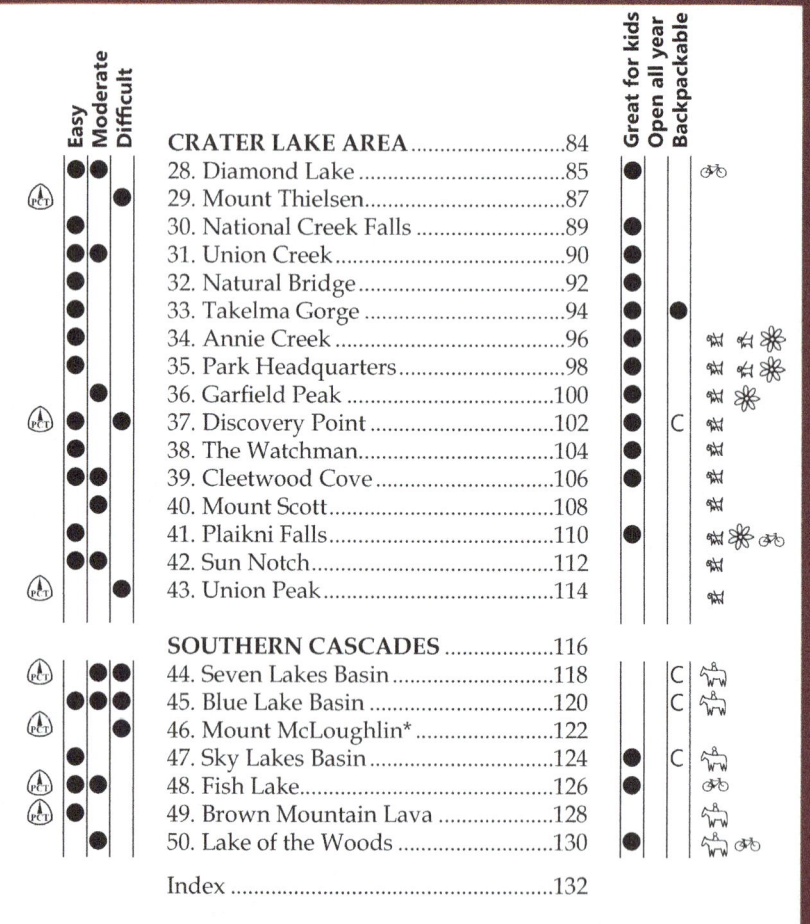

	Easy	Moderate	Difficult				Great for kids	Open all year	Backpackable	

CRATER LAKE AREA 84
28. Diamond Lake 85
29. Mount Thielsen 87
30. National Creek Falls 89
31. Union Creek 90
32. Natural Bridge 92
33. Takelma Gorge 94
34. Annie Creek 96
35. Park Headquarters 98
36. Garfield Peak 100
37. Discovery Point 102
38. The Watchman 104
39. Cleetwood Cove 106
40. Mount Scott 108
41. Plaikni Falls 110
42. Sun Notch 112
43. Union Peak 114

SOUTHERN CASCADES 116
44. Seven Lakes Basin 118
45. Blue Lake Basin 120
46. Mount McLoughlin* 122
47. Sky Lakes Basin 124
48. Fish Lake 126
49. Brown Mountain Lava 128
50. Lake of the Woods 130

Index 132

KEY TO MAP SYMBOLS

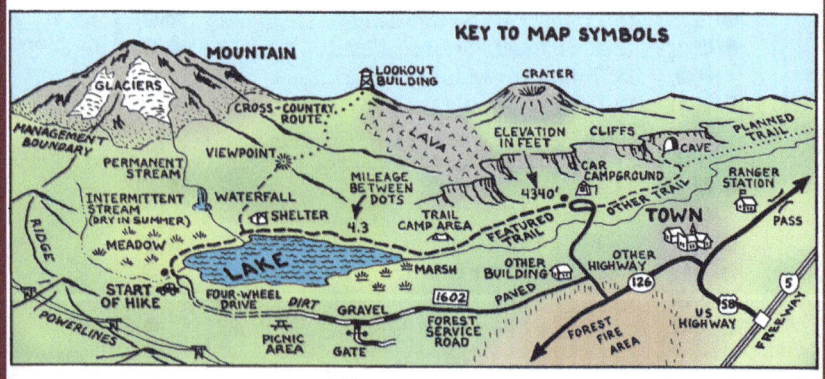

- Horses OK   - Bicycles OK   - Dogs on leash   - No pets
- Wildflowers (count petals for peak month)   *NW Forest Pass site   **Other parking fee
- C - Crowded or restricted backpacking area   - Pacific Crest Trail   - Rough access road

Highlights of the
ROGUE VALLEY

Lower Rogue River
Famed for its whitewater, this mischievous river actually has many moods. It begins at springs near Crater Lake, churns underground through a lava tube (Hike #32), lazes past the Medford area's Table Rocks (Hike #1), and finally roars through a wilderness canyon (see page 16). Hikers trace this western segment on a 40-mile trail (Hikes #26 and #27) while others brave the rapids by raft or kayak.

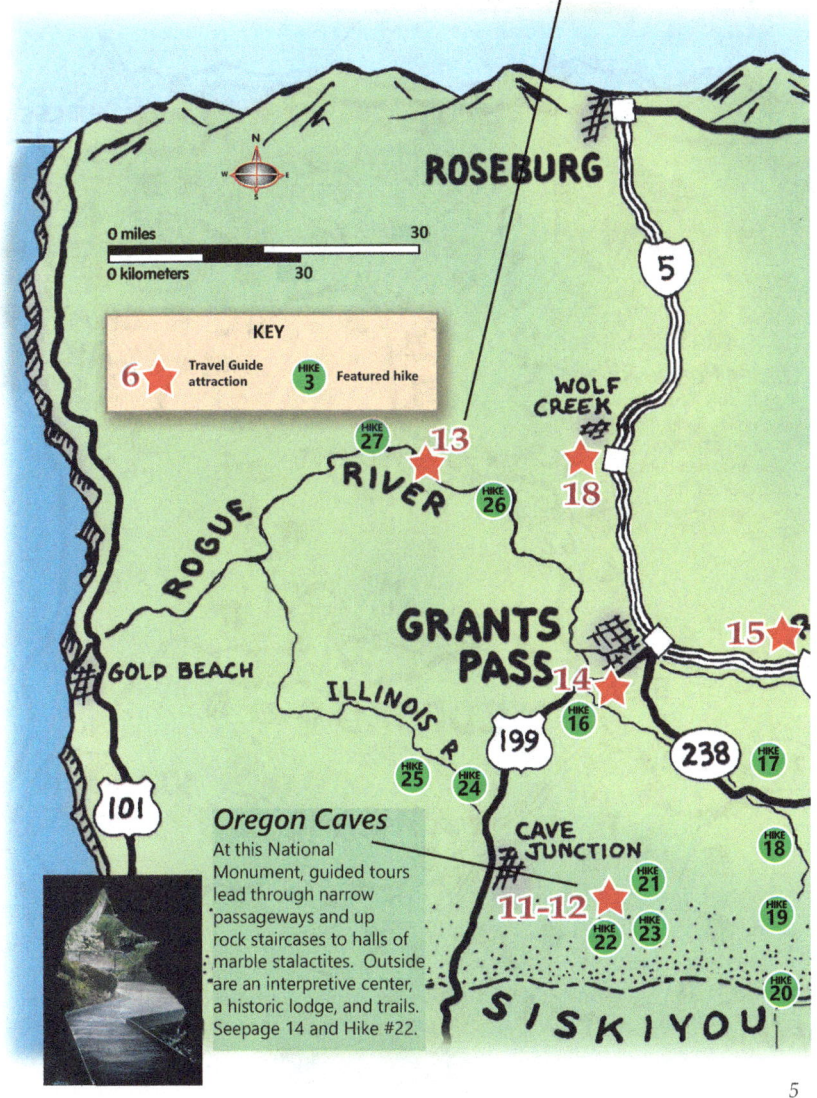

Oregon Caves
At this National Monument, guided tours lead through narrow passageways and up rock staircases to halls of marble stalactites. Outside are an interpretive center, a historic lodge, and trails. See page 14 and Hike #22.

5

Crater Lake

Most visitors to this National Park merely drive along the rim to viewpoints. Stop at historic Crater Lake Lodge (page 8), where a trail leads to a view atop Garfield Peak (Hike #36). The only access to the lake itself is a 1.1-mile path down to Cleetwood Cove (Hike #39), where you can catch a boat tour around Wizard Island (see page 10). Snow closes the 33-mile Rim Drive from November to July, but you can still drive up to the Rim Village for a look.

Upper Rogue River

At its headwaters near Crater Lake, this rushing mountain river foams through a rock gorge and then ducks underground in a lava tunnel (Hikes #32-33),

Ashland

This college town hosts a world-class theater festival from March to October. Upscale galleries, brewpubs, and bed & breakfast inns fill the city. See pages 18-19.

At Crater Lake's Rim Village, descend a stone staircase behind the Rim Visitor Center to find the Sinnott Memorial Overlook, a viewpoint building with exhibits and 20-minute ranger talks in summer.

A Visit to
CRATER LAKE

Crater lake fills the caldera of Mount Mazama, a volcano that collapsed in a cataclysimic eruption in 5677 BC. The explosion blew 12 cubic miles of rock into the sky. The deepest lake in North America, Crater Lake has no outlet but maintains its level by evaporation and seepage. The lake's purity and 1943-foot depth account for its stunning blue color.

Klamath tribal legends claim the lake is the haunt of an evil spirit named Llao. Native Americans refused to speak of the lake, so it was not discovered early by white explorers. National Park status came in 1902.

The park receives an average of 44 feet of snow each winter. Only the south access road from Highway 62 to the Rim Village is plowed. Mazama Village, open from mid-June through September, has a campground, grocery store, gas station, and motel.

A few National Park rules: Pets are permitted only on leash in developed areas, and are not allowed on trails. Horses are limited to the Pacific Crest Trail, and grazing is banned. If you're backpacking, pick up the required, free backcountry camping permit at park headquarters.

From Medford, follow "Crater Lake" signs on Highway 62 for 73 miles and turn left to the park's entrance booth. Expect to pay $30 per car here for a 7-day pass ($15 in winter). Then continue seven miles to Rim Village.

Trolleys leave Rim Village for 2-hour guided tours around Rim Drive hourly beginning at 10am from July to mid-September. Tickets are $29 for adults and $18 for kids.

Waiters serve drinks and snacks to visitors in the rocking chairs on the lodge's terrace.

1 CRATER LAKE LODGE

Crater Lake's grand old lodge was not always grand. Built between 1909 and 1915 for just $50,000, it originally opened with tarpaper on its outside walls and flimsy beaverboard between rooms. After years of neglect, it was slated for

Garfield Peak rises behind Crater Lake Lodge.

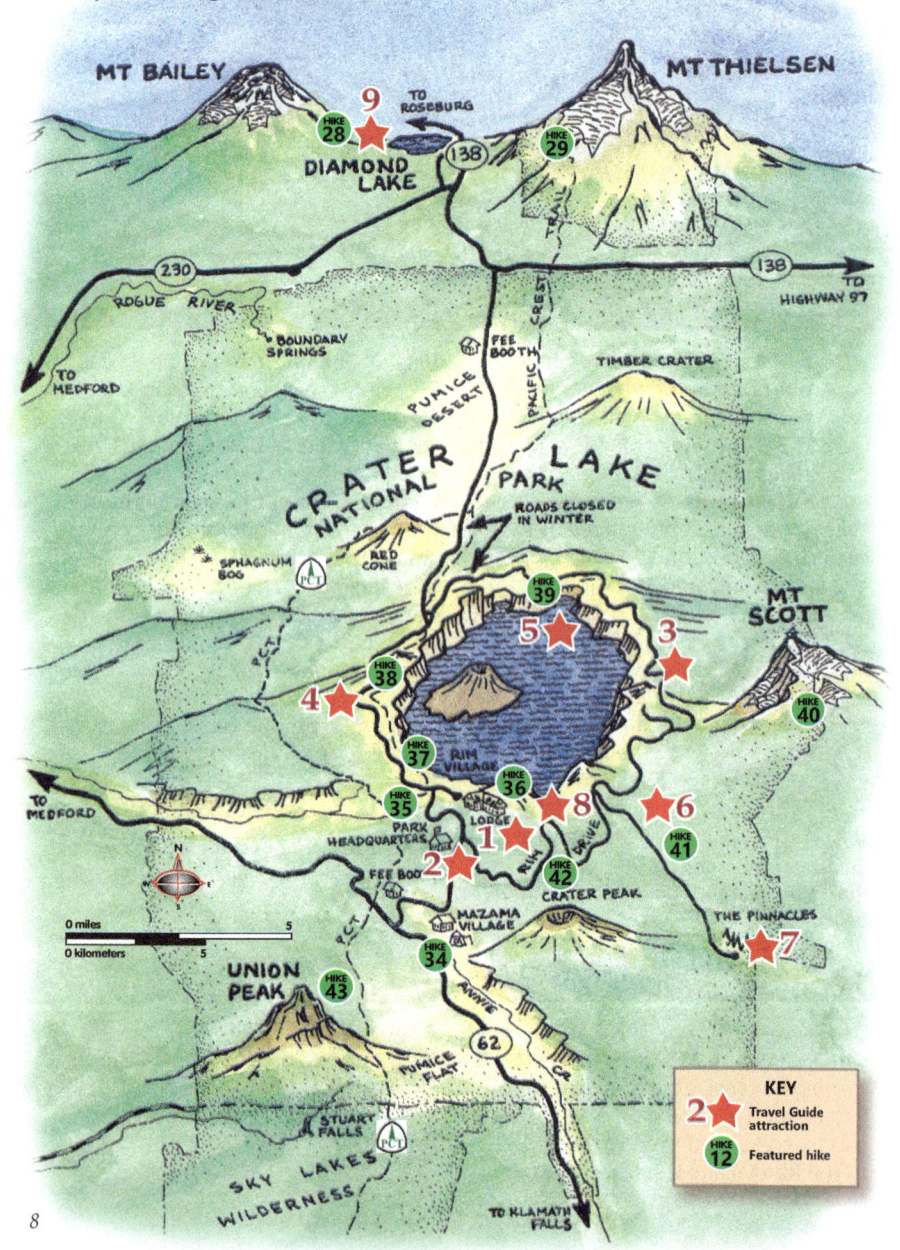

KEY
★ Travel Guide attraction
● Featured hike

8

Cedar bark adorns the lodge's Great Hall.

demolition in the 1980s, but a public outcry pushed the Park Service to spend $35 million renovating it instead.

The rebuilt lodge still has a rustic ambiance, with finely crafted stone walls and woodwork. All 71 of the guest rooms now have private baths. Reservations are essential in the elegant dining room, but you can order the same menu, without reservations, from the comfortable chairs of the Great Hall or patio.

For less spendy fare, follow a scenic walk along the lake's rim to a gift shop and cafe at the other end of the Rim Village. Along the way you'll pass a Visitor Center where friendly rangers answer questions about the park.

Crater Lake Lodge is open from mid-May to mid-October. For reservations see *explorecraterlake.com*. To find the lodge from the Crater Lake turnoff on Highway 62, drive 7 miles north to the Rim Village and keep right for 0.3 mile to a parking turnaround.

2 PARK HEADQUARTERS

Open year-round, the Steel Information Center at park headquarters has helpful rangers, a 16-minute movie, and a selection of books and gifts. Hours are 9am to 5pm (10am to 4pm in winter).

The Information Center was built as a dormitory in 1936.

Two short walks begin here. A 0.5-mile path loops past the historic park headquarters buildings along Munson Creek. Across the road, a 0.4-mile trail leads to the 0.4-mile Castle Crest wildflower loop. See Hike #35. To find Park Headquarters, drive 4 miles north from the Crater Lake turnoff of Highway 62, or 3 miles south from Rim Village.

Stepping stones on the Castle Crest loop trail accesss Munson Creek's wildflowers.

From Crater Lake Lodge, a popular trail (Hike #36) climbs Garfield Peak to one of the best viewpoints of the lake.

3 RIM DRIVE

The spectacular 33-mile loop road around Crater Lake's rim passes dozens of viewpoint pullouts and several picnic areas. It's also the only access for Cleetwood Cove's boat tours *(see below)* and many of the park's best hiking trails. Plan at least half a day to complete the circuit.

Two bulldozers begin clearing the Rim Drive of snowdrifts in April, but the loop seldom opens before early July. Fresh snow closes it again after October.

Start the loop either at Rim Village or at a junction near park headquarters.

Built in 1931-32, The Watchman's lookout has a small museum in its basement.

5 BOAT TOURS

The most popular path in Crater Lake National Park—and the only allowed route to the lake itself—is the switchbacking 1.1-mile trail descending from Rim Drive down to Cleetwood Cove's tour boat dock (Hike #39).

The trail and the boat tours are open from early July to early September in 2025, but will be entirely closed in 2026 and 2027 while the dock and trail are reconstructed to improve safety and protect the environment. When the trail reopens in July 2028 the ticket office will be located by the rebuilt dock and

The Watchman's lookout (Hike #38) has the park's best view of Wizard Island.

4 THE WATCHMAN

Just 4 miles north of Rim Village, Rim Drive passes a notch in the rim with an aerial view of Wizard Island. Stop here for a look at the volcanic cinder cone named for its resemblance to a sorcerer's hat. The view is even better if you hike a steep 0.8-mile trail up to The Watchman's patio at a historic fire lookout tower. The path gains 420 feet of elevation, climbing through a sparse forest of storm-stunted whitebark pines. See Hike #38.

The only access to Crater Lake's popular boat tours is the switchbacking 1.1-mile Cleetwood Cove Trail (Hike #39).

new restroom facilities at the bottom of the trail, rather than at the trailhead on Rim Drive.

The standard boat tour (about $50 for adults and $35 for children age 3-12) takes two hours, visiting Wizard Island and looping back past Phantom Ship as park rangers describe the sights. Boats that visit only Wizard Island sail at 9am and 11:30am and cost a little less.

Some boat tours dock at Wizard Island.

Pack a warm coat and possibly an umbrella, because the 40-seat boats have no roofs. Pets are not permitted. Check *explorecraterlake.com/things-to-do/boat-tours/* for schedules and reservations.

To find the trailhead from Crater Lake's Rim Village, take Rim Drive clockwise 10.6 miles to the trailhead. If you're coming from the park's north entrance off Highway 138, turn left along Rim Drive for 4.6 miles.

Llao Rock, a cliff on the tour boat route.

Plaikni Falls waters a glen of wildflowers.

❻ PLAIKNI FALLS

The newest trail at Crater Lake is already the second most popular. An easy 1-mile path leads to a wildflower glen by a small waterfall. To find it from park headquarters, take East Rim Drive 8.5 miles (counter-clockwise around the lake) and turn right on Pinnacles Road for a mile. See Hike #41.

WHITEBARK PINES

The bent, struggling trees you see at timberline at Crater Lake are whitebark pines. These five-needle pines grow only above 7000 feet. Their amazingly supple limbs allow them to bend, rather than break, in winter gales. The seeds are a favorite food of Clark's nutcrackers. By flying from peak to peak with the seeds, this bird helps whitebark pines spread.

Whitebark pine branches are so flexible they can be tied in knots.

7 THE PINNACLES

Spires of welded ash rise from a canyon that was buried during Crater

Mt. Scott looms above the ash pinnacles of Wheeler Creek's canyon (see Hike #41).

CRATER LAKE IN WINTER

Skiing around Crater Lake's snowed-under Rim Drive is a rugged 33-mile trek, best undertaken in March or April.

For an easier tour, join a ranger-led, 2-hour showshoe walk around Rim Village at 1pm any Saturday or Sunday from December through March. The tours are free — even snowshoes are provided — but sign up first at park headquarters or call 541-594-3100.

Skiing around the lake takes 3 days.

Lake's eruption 7700 years ago. Take Rim Drive east of park headquarters 8.5 miles and turn right on paved Pinnacles Road 7 miles to road's end.

8 PHANTOM SHIP

A small craggy island at the foot of Dutton Cliff *(below)*, Phantom Ship is a fragment of a volcano that predated the eruptions that began creating ancient Mount Mazama 400,000 years ago. The boat tour loops around the island, but to see its other moods *(at right)*, hike a half-mile loop path from the Rim Drive to an overlook at Sun Notch. See Hike #42.

⑨ Diamond Lake

Why do twice as many Oregonians visit Diamond Lake as the more famous Crater Lake National Park a few miles to the south? Both lakes have mountain views, but Diamond Lake's shore is more accessible, with over 400 campsites, five boat ramps, a resort lodge, and a paved 11.5-mile loop trail.

Diamond Lake has an average depth of only 20 feet, so it becomes swimmably warm in August. It's also heavily stocked to provide catchable trout. When fishing is best in June and early July, mosquitoes can be thick.

Diamond Lake Lodge.

Start your visit at Diamond Lake Lodge. The compound includes not only a restaurant and store, but also a marina shop where you can rent boats and bicycles. If you're hiking, simply walk to the sandy picnic beach in front of the lodge, follow the lakeshore to the right, climb to the paved bike path, and stroll as far as you like. See Hike #28.

The Rogue River Trail near Union Creek.

⑩ Union Creek

The upper Rogue River briefly vanishes underground near this woodsy resort village. The secret behind the river's stunt is an ancient lava tube, left from flows that poured down this river valley from Crater Lake's volcano.

On Highway 62 west of Crater Lake 20 miles (or northeast of Medford 56 miles), Union Creek is a very rustic place, with an old-timey general store, an ice cream shop, rentable cabins, and a campground built by the Civilian Conservation Corps in the 1930s.

A few hundred yards north of town on Highway 62, park at the Rogue Gorge viewpoint to see the river churn through a collapsed lava tube.

To see the river sucked into an intact cave, drive the highway south of town a mile, turn right toward Natural Bridge Campground, and keep left for 0.7 mile. See Hike #32.

Left: The paved bike path around Diamond Lake has views of spire-topped Mt. Thielsen.

13

A Visit to Oregon Caves

Poet Joaquin Miller's praise of the "great Marble Halls of Oregon" helped win National Monument status for Oregon Caves in 1909. Underground tours now visit the cave formations, but the national monument has been expanded, so there's a lot to do above ground as well.

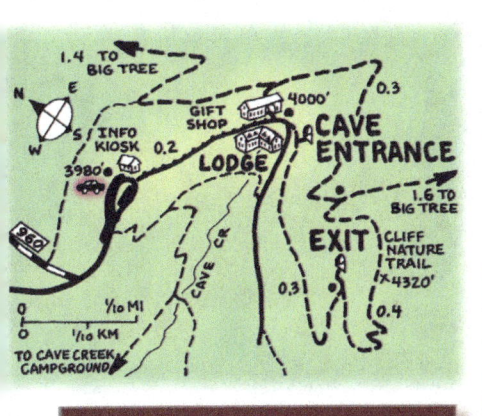

quickest return route is a 0.3-mile trail to the right. See Hike #22.

To find Oregon Caves, drive Highway 199 south from Grants Pass for 29 miles to Cave Junction and follow "Oregon Caves" pointers east on Highway 46 for 20 miles to a turnaround. Park here and walk up the road 0.2 mile to the gift shop and cave entrance on the left.

11 Cave Tours

Cave tours leave about every half hour from 9am to 6pm in summer, and about every hour from 10am to 4pm in spring and fall. There are no tours from early November to late March.

You don't need a flashlight, but because it averages 44° F in the cave year-round, you'll want warm clothes. The 90-minute tour climbs 0.6 mile through the cave to an upper exit. From there the

The Chateau's patio overlooks a waterfall.

Across from the cave entrance is the 1934 Chateau, a lodge sided with cedar bark.

12 And Above Ground

The Chateau, a 1934 lodge in the grand tradition of the National Parks, stands opposite the cave entrance. In addition to more than 20 rooms, the Chateau has a 1930s-style coffee shop, a restaurant with a mountain stream, and a historic lounge open to the public. Closed in 2020 for restoration, The Chateau is otherwise open from early May to early October. For reservations call 541-592-3400 or check *oregoncaveschateau.com*.

Five hiking trails start near the Chateau. For a 3.3-mile loop, cross the street and walk through the visitor center's breeezeway. The Big Tree Loop climbs past wildflowers to a giant Douglas fir (see Hike #22).

15

The Rogue River stands on edge in the narrows of Mule Creek Canyon.

An easy 2.1-mile walk from the Grave Creek Bridge leads to Rainie Falls, where boaters stop to portage. (Hike #26).

13 THE ROGUE RIVER

Snaking from Crater Lake National Park to the sea, the Rogue River crosses the heart of Southern Oregon. To see the scenic river at its best, detour off Interstate 5 just north of Grants Pass at exit 61. Drive 4 miles west to Merlin and follow the river downstream 14 miles to the Smullin Visitor Center at Rand, where rangers offer travel tips. Good advice is to continue driving downriver another 4.5 miles to the Grave Creek Bridge, where whitewater boaters (and hikers) launch into the river's wildest canyon, a 40-mile stretch too rugged for roads. An easy 2.1-mile walk samples that canyon as far as Rainie Falls (see Hike #26).

Floating the 40 miles from Grave Creek to Illahee is a world-class 3-day whitewater trip. A commercially guided trip with overnight stays at private lodges costs about $1000-1600 per person. If you'd rather raft the Rogue on your own, you'll need a permit during the restricted season from May 15 to October 15. Permits are hard to get, chosen by lottery between Dec. 1 and Feb. 1. For information, check "Lotteries" at **www.recreation.gov**.

Left: Flora Dell Falls, beside the Rogue River Trail. Below: The Coffeepot swirls boats in Mule Creek Canyon.

16

14 GRANTS PASS

With an arch across its main downtown street proclaiming "It's the Climate!" this city on the Rogue River has long been a haven for retirees seeking warmth. But it has also become a center for whitewater rafters and artists. See the river beside the **Taprock Northwest Grill** (971 SE 6th), between the bridges of 6th and 7th Streets. See the art at the **Bear Hotel,** a warehouse of bizarre fiberglass sculptures, open by appointment on weekdays. Call the Evergreen Bank at 541-479-3351 to schedule a visit.

The Rogue River in downtown Grants Pass.

15 OREGON VORTEX

This hokey 1930 roadside attraction is a fun diversion from a drive on Interstate 5. For $13.95 ($9.75 for kids age 6-11) a guide takes you to a crooked 1905 shed where "everyday physical facts are reversed." Open March 1 to October 31. Midway between Grants Pass and Medford, take Gold Hill exits 40 or 43.

The Oregon Vortex, a "whirlpool of force."

The 1856 Bella Union Restaurant is one of a row of porched shops along California Street in Jacksonville's historic downtown.

16 JACKSONVILLE

This well-preserved gold mining boomtown from the 1800s is more than just a living museum; it's an active cultural center with art galleries and a first-rate summer music festival.

Miners on their way to California's more famous Gold Rush discovered gold here in Rich Gulch in 1852. The tent-and-plank town that sprang up was briefly Oregon's largest. After the easy gold was panned out, giant hydraulic hoses washed away acres of land in search of gold dust. Some locals later planted fruit orchards.

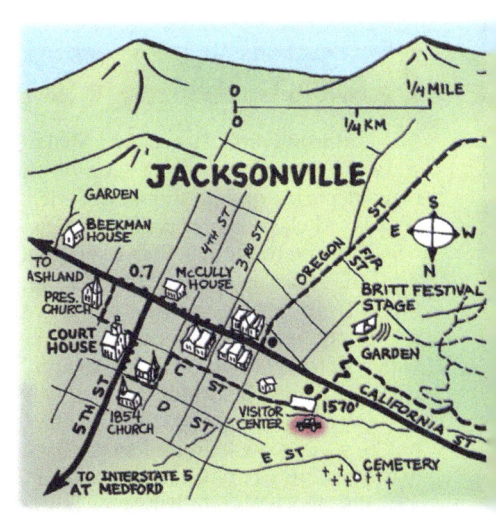

When the railroad bypassed Jacksonville in favor of Medford in 1886, the city slipped into a kind of suspended animation. To find Jacksonville from Interstate 5, take Medford exit 30 and follow signs 7 miles on Highway 238. At a "Britt Parking" sign opposite the 1883 county courthouse (now city hall), turn right on C Street for four blocks to its end at a visitor center.

The 1881 Presbyterian Church in Jacksonville.

For a quick tour, stroll California Street through town. For the area's best coffee, detour half a block up Oregon Street to the **Good-Bean Coffee Company**. For reasonably priced food and local brew, don't miss the restored 1856 **Bella Union Restaurant** on California Street. See also Hike #15.

The 1860 McCully House.

17 ASHLAND

This little university town has a Shakespearean theme, charming visitors with elegant parks, quaint shops, galleries, and world-class theater performances.

Start at the triangular **Plaza**, where a drinking fountain spouts **Lithia Water.** Piped from nearby springs as part of a 1914 spa scheme, this bubbly, bitter water contains lithium, sodium, calcium, iron, "and other healthful minerals."

A row of upscale shops faces the Plaza, but be sure to walk around to the back of this historic city block to see the open-air cafes and brewpub balconies lining

SHAKESPEARE FESTIVAL

Ashland college professor Angus Bowmer converted an abandoned lecture hall into a replica of Shakespeare's open-air Globe theater in 1935, launching a tradition of performing plays beside Lithia Park.

Today Ashland's Shakespearean Festival has blossomed into a world-class theater event, performing a

Ashland's open-air Elizabethan Stage.

dozen plays each year, including world premieres by modern playwrights. The 600-seat Bowmer Theatre and the 300-seat New Theatre host plays from March through October. The 1200-seat, open-air Elizabethan Stage *(above)* operates on summer evenings and cancels in case of rain.

Tudor banner in Ashland.

Tickets run $30-135. Sell-outs are common, so make reservations well in advance at 800-219-8161.

Check *www.osfashland.org* for the current play list, or drop by the box office at 15 South Pioneer Street, one block south of the Plaza. A tip if you can't get reservations: When the box office opens at 9:30am, unclaimed tickets for that day's plays are offered for sale.

Catering to theater crowds, Ashland has more bed & breakfast inns than Portland.

A fountain in the Plaza dispenses bitter Lithia water from a carbonated spring.

Ashland Creek. An outdoor crafts fair sets up on the creekside promenade on summer weekends.

Then stroll upstream through **Lithia Park**, in a woodsy canyon with duck-filled lakes, playgrounds, flowerbeds, and the cascades of Ashland Creek. The park extends a mile upstream (Hike #6).

Next return to the Plaza and head south through **downtown** on East Main Street for window shopping. A favorite haunt of locals is **Bloomsbury Books** (290 E. Main) with its upstairs coffee house. Another favorite is the **Northwest Nature Shop**, a block south of Main at 154 Oak Street.

From Interstate 5, take Ashland exit 14 or 19 and follow signs 2.5 miles.

An 1883 stagecoach stop, now by a freeway.

Ashland's downtown.

18 WOLF CREEK INN

Jack London and Clark Gable stayed at this 1883 "tavern," a stagecoach stop on the route of the Applegate's 1846 Oregon Trail. Off Interstate 5 at Wold Creek exit 76 (south of Roseburg 48 miles or north of Grants Pass 18 miles), the hotel offers 5 historic rooms, a first-rate restaurant, and paranormal tours. Reservations: 541-866-2474 or *wolfcreekinn.com*.

WILDLIFE OF SOUTHERN OREGON

Oregon's black bears are smaller and less aggressive than grizzlies, but they do scavenge unsecured food.

Coyotes are much smaller than wolves, and are driven out in wolves' range.

Wolves have reestablished packs in the Southern Oregon Cascades, but are very shy.

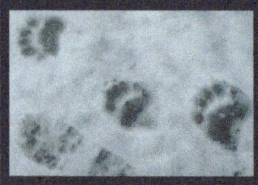

Black bear tracks in the snow.

Raccoons are occasional night visitors.

American martens hunt chipmunks and squirrels.

Cougars (mountain lions) are shy and nocturnal, so they are rarely seen.

Bobcats are nocturnal, so people rarely see them in Oregon.

Mule deer are much smaller than elk, and have large ears.

Porcupines are slow and unaggressive, but often hurt dogs that attack them.

Elk can weigh 1000 pounds.

Great-horned owls roost on tree limbs by day and hunt by night.

Pikas live in alpine rockslides.

Golden-mantled ground squirrels are larger than chipmunks and don't have an eye stripe.

The gray jay or "camp robber" boldly swoops to picnic tables for food scraps. Don't feed them! Human food can hurt wild animals.

Marmots are larger than pikas. They live in timberline rockslides and whistle when alarmed.

Townsend's chipmunk.

The Clark's nutcracker uses its bill to open whitebark pine nuts near timberline.

LOWLAND WILDFLOWERS

OOKOW *(Dichelostemma congestum)* blooms in dry, grassy meadows from April to June.

INDIAN WARRIOR *(Pedicularis densiflora).* This snapdragon relative blooms in April and May.

FIREWEED *(Epilobium angustifolium).* After a fire, this plant crowds slopes with tall pink spires.

WILD IRIS *(Iris tenax).* Also called an Oregon flag, this June bloom varies from blue to yellow-white.

PRAIRIE STAR *(Lithophragma parviflora)* blooms in May in dry, rocky fields and slopes.

FOXGLOVE *(Digitalis purpurea).* Showy 5-foot foxglove stalks spangle sunny summer hillsides.

ELEGANT BRODIAEA *(Brodiaea elegans)* blooms in dry grasslands in early summer.

PITCHER PLANT *(Darlingtonia californica),* a bog-dweller, traps and dissolves insects for fertilizer.

SALSIFY *(Tragopogon dubius).* This dry June roadside flower turns to a giant dandelion-like seed puffball.

BACHELOR BUTTON *(Centaurea cyanus).* One of many showy blue composite flowers with this name.

DEATH CAMAS *(Zigadenus spp.).* Dangerously similar to edible camas, this bloom's root is poison.

FAREWELL TO SPRING *(Clarkia amoena).* This Clarkia blooms in dry grasslands as summer arrives.

MEADOW WILDFLOWERS

WILD ONION *(Allium spp.)*. This pungent bloom hugs the ground in dry, rocky areas.

LARKSPUR *(Delphinium menziesii)*. Stalks of larkspur stand up to two feet tall in meadows.

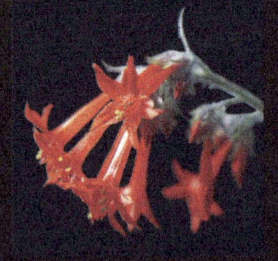

SCARLET GILIA or SKYROCKET *(Gilia aggregata)* blooms on dry, open slopes all summer.

HELLEBORE or CORN LILY *(Veratrum insolitum)* has poison roots and 4-foot stalks of green flowers.

BIGELOW SNEEZEWEED *(Helenium bigelovii)*. These bulbous blooms grow near timberline.

JACOB'S LADDER *(Polemonium occidentale)*, often pale blue, likes damp spots in high forests.

INDIAN CARTWHEEL *(Silene hookeri)*. Also called stringflower, this bloom likes dry rocky ground.

FRITILLARY *(Fritillaria spp.)*. This odd, nodding brown "chocolate lily" likes subalpine meadows.

SHOOTING STAR *(Dodecatheon jeffreyi)*. Early in summer, shooting stars carpet wet fields and slopes.

MOUNTAIN BLUEBELL *(Mertensia spp.)*. A favorite browse for elk, these fill subalpine meadows.

STONECROP *(Sedum oreganum)*. This plant survives in rocky ground by storing water in fat leaves.

CONEFLOWER (Rudbeckia occidentalis). Like a petalless daisy, coneflower grows waist-high.

FOREST WILDFLOWERS

COLUMBINE *(Aquilegia formosa)*. In wet woodlands, this bloom has nectar lobes for hummingbirds.

FAIRY BELLS *(Disporum hookeri)*. This lily of moist woodlands later develops pairs of orange berries.

OREGON GRAPE *(Berberis aquifolium)*. Oregon's state flower has holly-like leaves and blue berries.

SOURGRASSS *(Oxalis oregana)*. Shamrock-shaped leaves carpet forests and have a tart taste.

FAIRY SLIPPER *(Calypso bulbosa)*. This lovely 6-inch orchid haunts the mossy floor of old forests.

PRINCE'S PINE *(Chimaphila umbellata)*. Also known as pipsissewa, this blooms in shade.

BLEEDING HEART *(Dicentra formosa)*. Look near woodland creeks for these pink hearts.

TWINFLOWER *(Linnaea borealis)*. This double bloom grows in the far North around the globe.

CANDYFLOWER *(Claytonia sibirica)*. Common by woodland trails, candyflower is edible.

STAR-FLOWERED SOLOMONSEAL *(Maianthemum stellata)*. Delicate stars decorate deep forests.

WESTERN AZALEA *(Rhododendron occidentale)* blooms in May near the Southern Oregon Coast.

TRILLIUM *(Trillium ovatum)*. This spectacular woodland lily blooms in April, a herald of spring.

ALPINE WILDFLOWERS

PHLOX *(Phlox diffusa)*. A colorful cushion, phlox hugs arid rock outcrops with a mat of blooms.

PAINTBRUSH *(Castilleja spp.)* has showy red-orange sepals, but the actual flowers are green tubes.

PENSTEMON *(Penstemon spp.)*. Look for these red, purple, or blue trumpets in high, rocky areas.

ELEPHANTS HEAD *(Pedicularis groenlandica)*. You'll see pink elephants like this in alpine bogs.

ASTER *(Aster spp.)*. This purple daisy-like flower blooms late in summer, from July to September.

FAWN LILY *(Erythronium spp.)*. These 6-petaled lilies erupt a week after the snow melts.

BEARGRASS *(Xerophyllum tenax)* resembles a giant bunchgrass until it blooms with a tall, lilied plume.

LUPINE *(Lupinus spp.)* has fragrant blooms in early summer and pea-pod-shaped fruit in fall.

MONKEYFLOWER *(Mimulus spp.)*. Clumps of these showy pink or yellow flowers line alpine brooks.

GENTIAN *(Gentiana calycosa)*. These thumb-sized blooms near alpine lakes open only in full sun.

WESTERN PASQUE FLOWER *(Anemone occidentalis)*. This high alpine flower *(left)* blooms so early it sometimes melts holes in the snow. By August it develops foot-tall, dishmop-shaped seedheads *(right)*.

Introduction

Welcome to the recreation playground of Southern Oregon! This guidebook features trails for day hikers, mountain bikers, dog walkers, equestrians, backpackers, and hikers with kids.

HOW TO USE THIS BOOK

It's Easy to Choose a Trip
To quickly find an outing to match your tasts, look for the following symbols beside the hikes' headings.

    Children's favorites — walks popular with the 4- to 12-year-old crowd, but fun for hikers of all ages.

    All-year trails, hikable most or all of winter.   Wildflowers.

    Hikes suitable for backpackers as well as day hikers.

    Crowded or restricted backpacking areas.

    Dogs on leash.   No pets.   Rough access road.

The Information Blocks
Each hike is rated by difficulty. **Easy** hikes are between 1 and 6 miles round trip and gain less than 800 feet in elevation. Never very steep nor particularly remote, they make good warm-up trips for experienced hikers or first-time trips for novices.

Trips rated as **Moderate** range from 2 to 9 miles round trip. The longer hikes in this category are not steep, but shorter trails may gain up to 1600 feet of elevation — or they may require some pathfinding skills. Hikers must be in good condition and will need to take several rest stops.

Difficult trails demand top physical condition, with a strong heart and strong knees. These challenging hikes are 6 to 20 miles round-trip and may gain 3000 feet or more. Backpacking can break difficult hikes into manageable segments.

Distances are given in round-trip mileage, except for those trails where a car or bicycle shuttle is so convenient that the suggested hike is one-way only, and is listed as such.

Elevation gains tell much about the difficulty of a hike. Those who puff climbing a few flights of stairs may consider even 500 feet of elevation a strenuous climb, and should watch this listing carefully. Note that the figures are for each hike's *cumulative* elevation gain, adding all the uphill portions, even those on the return trip.

The **hiking season** of any trail varies with the weather. In a cold year, a trail described as "Open May through October" may not yet be clear of snow by May 1, and may be socked in by a blizzard before October 31. Similarly, a trail that is "Open all year" may close due to storms.

The **allowed use** of some featured trails specifically includes horses and bicycle riders. Note that many of the hikes do not have a *use* listing at all. These are open to *hikers only*. For a quick overview of paths recommended for equestrians and mountain bikers, refer to the table of contents. The additional trails listed at the back of the book also include symbols identifying their allowed use.

Dogs are allowed on 39 of the 50 hikes, and leashes are required on 2 trails. Restrictions are noted both in the text and in the table of contents.

TOPOGRACHIC MAPS

All hikers in wilderness and other remote areas should carry a **topographic map**, with contour lines to show elevation. Topographic maps can be viewed for free at *mytopo.com* and many other Internet sites. Maps of Wilderness Areas can be purchased at outdoor stores or at the Northwest Nature Shop at 154 Oak Street in downtown Ashland. It also pays to pick up a National Forest road map, available at outdoor stores and ranger stations.

TRAILHEAD PARKING FEES

You'll need a **Northwest Forest Pass** to park within ¼ mile of the trailheads for Mt. Thielsen and Mt. McLoughlin. This permit costs $5 per car per day, or $30 per year, and can be purchased at ranger stations, outdoor stores, and some trailheads. For an "ePass" version, check *discovernw.org*. The pass is valid in National Forests throughout Oregon and Washington.

For trails inside Crater Lake National Park (Hikes #34-43), expect to pay a park entrance fee of $30 a car per week ($20 in winter).

Permit systems are subject to change, but hikes in this book currently requiring a pass are marked with an asterisk in the table of contents.

The Illinois River (Hike #25).

WILDERNESS RESTRICTIONS

Certain restrictions apply to designated Wilderness Areas, and affect many of the hikes featured in this guide:

- Groups must be no larger than 12.
- Campfires are discouraged, and are banned within 100 feet of any water source or maintained trail.
- Bicycles and other vehicles (except wheelchairs) are banned.
- Horses and pack stock cannot be tethered within 200 feet of any water source or shelter.
- Motorized equipment, drones, hang gliders, and fireworks are banned.
- Live trees and shrubs must not be cut or damaged.

In addition, some rules apply to all federal lands:
- Collecting arrowheads or other cultural artifacts is a federal crime.
- Permits are required to dig up plants.

SAFETY ON THE TRAIL

Wild Animals
Part of the fun of hiking is watching for wildlife. Lovers of wildness rue the demise of our most impressive species. Grizzly bears were driven to extinction in Southern Oregon long ago. The little black bears that remain are so profoundly shy you probably won't see one in years of hiking. To keep them shy, it's important for backpackers to hang food at least 10 feet high and 5 feet from a tree trunk at night. Only where cooler chest goodies are easily accessible have black bears become campground nuisances, particularly at Crater Lake, in Castle Crags State Park, and at river-rafting campsites on the Rogue River.

Statistically, rattlesnakes are less of a threat than horses, bees, dogs, or even cows. Nonetheless, if you hear a rattle or recognize the snake's diamondback pattern, it's your cue to give this reclusive animal some space.

Wolves returned to the Southern Oregon Cascades in 2013. They do not interact with people. Likewise cougars eat deer, but never eat people. To avoid confusion, do not imitate a deer by jogging or biking through the forest alone in the evening without a light.

Ticks can be carriers of Lyme disease, which begins with flu-like symptoms and an often circular rash. This is very rare in Oregon. Nonetheless, brush off your clothes and check under your collar and cuffs after walking through dry grass or brush.

Mosquitoes can be a nuisance on hikes in the Cascades, particularly in the Sky Lakes and Mt. Thielsen Wilderness Areas. To avoid them, remember that these insects hatch about ten days after the snow melts from the trails and that they remain in force about three weeks. Thus, if a given trail in the Cascades is listed as "Open mid-June," expect mosquitoes there most of July.

Drinking Water
Day hikers should bring all the water they will need—roughly a quart per person. A microscopic parasite, *Giardia*, has forever changed the old custom of dipping a drink from every brook. The symptoms of "beaver fever," debilitating nausea and diarrhea, commence a week or two after ingesting *Giardia*. If you're backpacking, bring an approved water filter or purification tablet, or boil your water 5 minutes.

Car Clouting
Parked cars at trailheads are sometimes the targets of *car clouters*, thieves who smash windows. The simplest solution is to leave no valuables in the car and to leave doors unlocked.

Proper Equipment
Even on the tamest hike a surprise storm or a wrong turn can suddenly make the gear you carry very important. Always bring a pack with the **ten essentials:** extra insulation (a warm coat, extra clothing), navigation aids (a map, topographic if possible, and a compass), extra drinking water, extra food, repair tools (knife, tape), a fire starter (butane lighter, waterproof matches), first aid supplies, a flashlight, sun protection (sunglasses, sunscreen), and shelter (a

waterproof jacket, large garbage bag, or space blanket).

Before leaving on a hike, tell someone where you are going so they can alert the county sheriff to begin a search if you do not return on time. If you're lost, stay put and keep warm. The number one killer in the woods is *hypothermia* – being cold and wet too long.

GLOBAL POSITIONING SYSTEMS (GPS)

Some of the hikes in this book include **GPS** notations, such as *42.0908 -123.0967*. The first number is the location's north latitude, and the second is its west longitude. This optional information may be used to pinpoint your location using a device that tracks satellite signals. If you have a smart phone, an app is an effective GPS tool. Remember to download free topo maps before your hike. A GPS device is not a substitute for a map and compass because batteries can fail and signals can be blocked. Also note that trail mileages computed by GPS devices may be inaccurate because they track a series of straight segments, not curves.

THE PACIFIC CREST TRAIL

The 2650-mile Pacific Crest Trail (PCT) from Mexico to Canada is one of the world's great athletic challenges. To follow it through Southern Oregon, look for PCT symbols beside hikes in the table of contents. Then flip to the specific hike descriptions, where you'll find PCT symbols in the margin highlighting each section of the trail. Although the maps do not always overlap, arrows at the edge of one map indicate the distance to PCT destinations on the next. For an overview of the entire route (without mileages), pick up a *PCT Southern Oregon* map at an outdoor store. Be aware that permits are required for many different parts of the PCT. If you're hiking very far it's simplest to get a single permit at *www.pcta.org*.

COURTESY ON THE TRAIL

As our trails become more heavily used, rules of trail etiquette become stricter:

- Pick no flowers.
- Leave no litter. Eggshells and orange peels can last for decades.
- Do not bring pets into wilderness areas. Dogs can frighten wildlife.
- Step off the trail on the downhill side to let horses pass. Speak to them quietly to help keep them from spooking.
- Do not shortcut switchbacks.

For backpackers, low-impact camping is essential, both to protect the landscape and to preserve a sense of solitude for others. The most important rules:

- Build no campfire. Cook on a backpacking stove.
- Wash 100 feet from any lake or stream.
- Camp on duff, rock, or sand – never on meadow vegetation.
- Pack out garbage – don't burn or bury it.

Medford Area

*Above: The Rogue Valley from Lower Table Rock near Medford (Hike #1).
Below: Jacksonville, a gold-mining boomtown from the 1800s (Hike #15).*

Hike 1

Table Rocks

Once a sanctuary for Takelma Indians, these two mesas near Medford are havens for hikers and endangered flowers.

Easy (Upper Table Rock)
2.8 miles round trip
720 feet elevation gain
Open all year,

Moderate (Lower Table Rock)
5.2 miles round trip
780 feet elevation gain

Trailheaad gate.

Views from the cliffs extend across the Rogue River to the Siskiyous and the Cascades. Visit in spring to catch the best flower displays and to avoid summer's merciless heat. Dogs, horses, firearms, fires, and flower picking are prohibited on both Table Rocks trails. Stay on designated paths to protect the fragile wildflowers.

An 1850 gold strike at Jacksonville attracted so many miners and settlers to the Rogue Valley that the local Takelma Indians launched attacks to reclaim their homeland. When the U.S. Army retaliated in 1853, the tribe retreated to Lower Table Rock, a natural fortress that long defied capture. The Takelmas were banished in 1856 to the Siletz Reservation on the northern Oregon Coast — but they still hold the Table Rocks sacred. In 2024 the Siletz Tribe bought 2000 acres here. Now they are working together with the Bureau of Land Management and the Nature Conservancy to preserve and restore the area.

Each mesa has its own trail. For information about the free, guided hikes led here on April and May weekends, call the Medford BLM office at 541-618-2200 or check *blm.gov/or/resources/recreation/tablerock*.

Getting There — Of the two trails, the path up Upper Table Rock is shorter and slightly easier. To find it from Interstate 5, take Central Point exit 33 just north of Medford, drive east on Biddle Road 1 mile, turn left on Table Rock Road for 5.2 miles to a curve, and turn right on Modoc Road for 1.5 miles to a parking lot on the left.

The Upper Table Rock Trail climbs through a scrub oak grassland ablaze with spring wildflowers. In all seasons, beware of triple-leafleted poison oak. At the 1.1-mile mark, after a final steep pitch, the trail suddenly emerges onto the table's amazingly flat, grassy summit. Continue straight across the mesa 0.3 mile to trail's end at a 200-foot cliff with a view west.

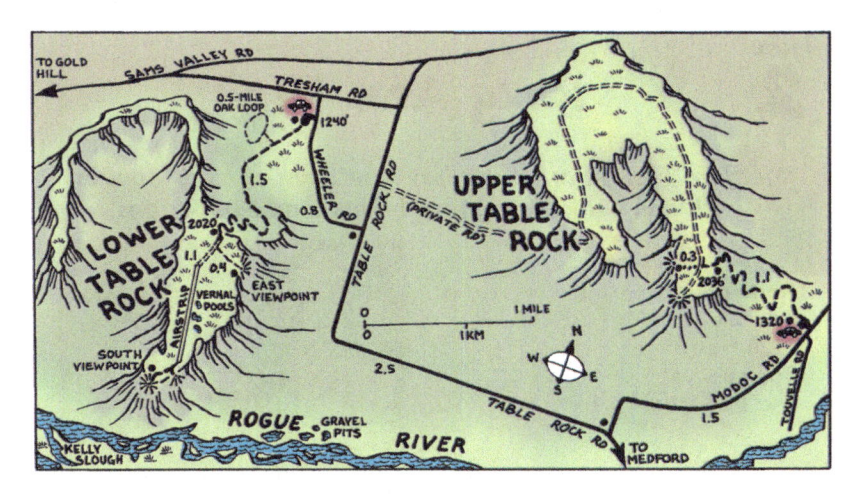

Although the trail to Lower Table Rock is longer and rockier, it climbs through shadier woods and leads to a taller cliff. To find this trailhead get back in your car, continue driving on Table Rock Road north of Medford to milepost 10 and turn left on Wheeler Road 0.8 mile. The trail sets off through grasslands with the same profusion of flowers as at the other mesa. The path climbs, steeply at times, through a dry forest of madrone and black oak. After 1.5 miles the path suddenly crests at the plateau and begins following an abandoned airstrip.

The quickest route to a viewpoint is to walk along the airstrip 0.1 mile and fork left on a trail 0.3 mile to a cliff. From here you can see your car far below. The snowy rim of Crater Lake rises above Upper Table Rock. The Rogue River, like a great green snake, curves across a quilt of orchards, ranches, and gravel pit ponds toward the distant white cone of Mt. McLoughlin. Turkey vultures soar on updrafts.

For the best view of all, however, hike back to the airstrip and follow it a mile across the mesa. On either hand you'll see vernal pools—ponds that dry up by May, leaving a haze of flowers. Look here for dwarf meadowfoam, a subspecies that exists only on the Table Rocks. At the airstrip's end, continue right on a path to a viewpoint overtowering the Rogue River.

Lower Table Rock.

Hike 2
Roxy Ann Peak

Medford's landmark butte has a network of trails popular with dog walkers, joggers, bikers, and equestrians.

Moderate
3.4-mile loop
1120 feet elevation gain
Open all year
Use: hikers, horses, bicycles

Trail signpost.

Despite its proximity to Medford, the steepish knoll in the middle of Prescott Park remains surprisingly wild. Atop Roxy Ann Peak you'll find oak woodlands, spring wildflowers, and a sweeping view across the Rogue River Valley to Mt. McLoughlin and the peaks of the Siskiyous.

Pioneer packers on the way to California in 1854 named Roxy Ann Peak for Roxana Baker, a nearby settler. In 1930 the Medford Lions Club donated 200 acres to launch the park, and Medford added 1500 acres the next year. When George Prescott, a Lions Club member, was shot in the line of duty as a policeman in 1937 the city named the park in his honor. In the 1930s Civilian Conservation Corps workers built trails, picnic areas, and roads to develop the park.

Although it's possible to drive to the summit, that track is so rough that it's closed in the wet months of winter and in the fire-hazard months of summer. Instead park at the entrance gate, where a path takes you to the summit viewpoint on a pleasant loop. Bikes are allowed on this loop, although it's recom-

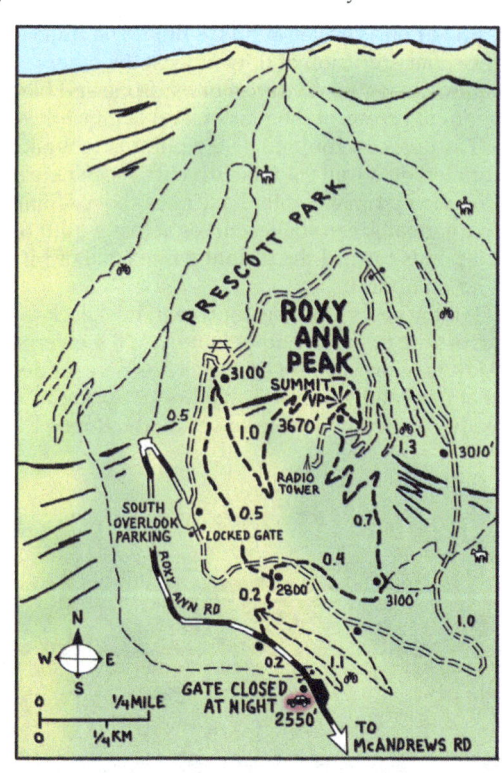

32

Historic picnic area sign halfway up Roxy Ann Peak.

mended that they return from the summit on a longer route to the east, via the zigzagging Rock and Roll Trail and Greenhorn Trail, marked with bicycle symbols on the map. Equestrians need to follow park roads and trails marked with a horse symbol.

Getting There— From Interstate 5 in Medford, take Biddle Road exit 30. Follow signs to take Biddle Road south beside the freeway for 0.8 mile. Then turn left on East McAndrews Road for 5.2 miles, keeping straight when the street changes names to Hillcrest Road. At a sign for Prescott Park turn left onto Roxy Ann Road for 0.2 mile of pavement and another 1.1 mile of gravel to a long parking pullout on the right, just before the park's second gate (locked at night).

Walk up the road 0.2 mile past the gate and turn uphill to the right on the Madrone Trail for 0.2 mile, ignoring the Greenhorn bicycle trail, to a fork at the start of the recommended loop. Veer left, crossing a dirt road to the Oak Trail.

The Oak Trail really does traverse a black oak grassland. You'll see a few stunted pines, lots of poison oak (stay on the trail!) and plenty of spring wildflowers. In May look for purple vetch, blue camas, fuzzy white cats ears, and yellow lomatium. Views extend across Medford to snowy Mt. Ashland.

After half a mile on the Oak Trail, turn uphill to the right on the Ponderosa Trail, which climbs for a mile on a long switchback up to a confusion of trails. Keep right at all junctions to find a picnic table on a rocky shoulder of Roxy Ann Peak's summit, with snowy Mt. McLoughlin on the horizon.

After soaking in the view, backtrack 40 feet and continue keeping right for 300 feet to a park road near the summit's radio tower, a popular roost for turkey vultures. For the hiking loop, walk back downhill on the road for 300 feet and turn right on the Manzanita Trail. Keeping right on this path for 1.1 mile will take you back to the start of the loop near your car.

If you're on a bicycle, however, don't take the Manzanita Trail. Instead continue down the summit road a few feet farther to the Rock and Roll Trail on the right. This path zooms down 1.3 miles, where you turn right on a gravel road for a mile and turn left on the Greenhorn Trail for another 1.1 mile to your car.

Hike 3
Grizzly Peak

Wildflowers, woodpeckers, and viewpoints highlight the loop around this high plateau near Ashland.

Easy
5.4-mile loop
750 feet elevation gain
Open mid-May to late November
Use: hikers, horses

Larkspur along the trail.

The loop trail traverses a fir forest with meadowed openings. A 2002 wildfire raced through the western third of the area, cleaning out smaller trees, opening new views, and leaving snags for woodpeckers. In 2017 Grizzly Peak was added to the Cascade-Siskiyou National Monument.

Getting There — Drive Interstate 5 to south Ashland exit 14, turn east toward Klamath Falls on Highway 66 for 0.7 mile, and turn left on Dead Indian Memorial Road for 6.7 miles. Turn left on Shale City Road for 3 miles, and then turn left on paved, pot-holed Road 38-2E-9.2. After 0.8 mile, keep straight at a three-way fork, continuing uphill another 0.8 mile to the trailhead at road's end *(GPS location 42.272 -122.6063)*.

The trail's first switchback above the parking lot has the area's best view east, sweeping from the snowy cone of Mt. McLoughlin to the distant Three Sisters. Beyond this the trail climbs gradually through a forest of Douglas fir and grand fir. Wildflowers carpet the forest floor in May and June: three-petaled white trilliums, yellow violets, and the large, ornate leaves of waterleaf. Later in summer, meadow slopes have stands of huge, 6-foot-tall blue larkspur.

Turn right at a fork after 1.2 miles, following a "Summit" pointer. But don't get excited about summiting this peak. When the path crests in another 0.3 mile, the

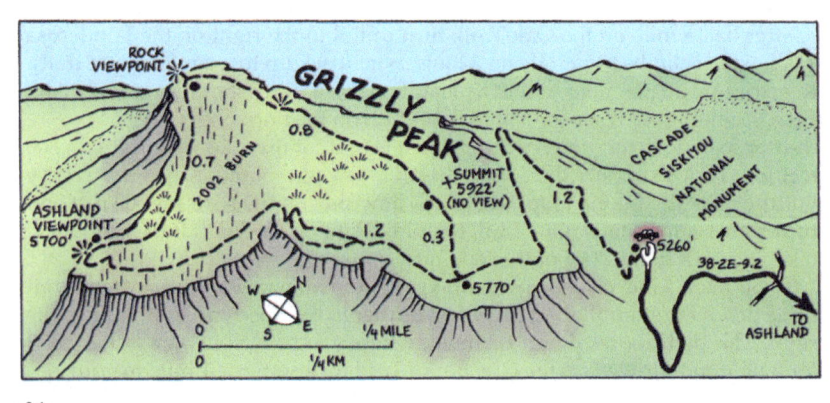

The view of Ashland from Grizzly Peak.   Below: Grizzly Peak from Ashland.

actual summit is a small, viewless rockpile 100 feet to the right. The chief attraction here is a surprise collection of pink wild onions, blooming from the gravel.

The rest of the hike has much better views, so sally onward along the loop trail. Soon you'll pass a large meadow, enter the fire zone, and begin tracing the rim of a broad plateau. The first views are north to Medford. Then a rock outcrop to the right overlooks Wagner Butte (Hike #11). The last viewpoint is the best of all, sweeping from the city of Ashland (on the right) to Mt. Ashland, Emigrant Lake, thumb-shaped Pilot Rock (Hike #5), and the ghostly cone of Mt. Shasta (on the left).

Follow the trail another 1.2 miles to complete the loop, and then keep right on the 1.2-mile path down to your car.

Hike 4 — Soda Mountain

The lookout atop this peak is the area's highest hiking goal, but wilder vistas await on quiet rock knolls nearby.

Easy (to Hobart Bluff)
2.4 miles round trip
300 feet elevation gain
Open June to mid-November
Use: hikers, horses

Moderate (to Soda Mountain)
3.9-mile loop
940 feet elevation gain

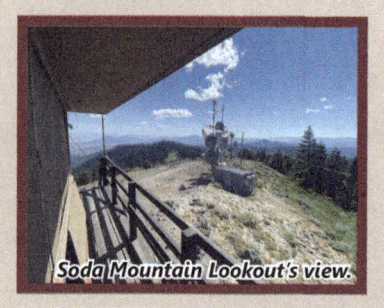

Soda Mountain Lookout's view.

    The Cascade-Siskiyou National Monument near Ashland not only commands dramatic views, but it also contains an intriguing mixture of plants. The Soda Mountain Wilderness, in the heart of the monument, stands at the junction of three biologic regions, where fir forests from the Cascades mingle with sagebrush from the High Desert and droopy incense cedars from the Siskiyous.
    The easiest hike from the trailhead is not actually to Soda Mountain, but rather in the opposite direction, on the Pacific Crest Trail to Hobart Bluff.
    Getting There — From Ashland exit 14 of Interstate 5, head east on Highway 66 toward Klamath Falls for 15 winding miles. Just before milepost 16, and immediately before the highway pass at Green Springs Mountain Summit, turn right on Soda Mountain Road 39-3E-32.3. Follow this one-lane gravel road 3.8 miles. The second time the road crosses under a set of big powerlines, park in the Hobart Bluff Trailhead with a restroom on the right, just beyond the powerlines (*GPS location 42.0852 -122.4817*). The Pacific Crest Trail crosses the road here.
    For the hike to Hobart Bluff, take the PCT north (to the *left* of the road), across a level meadow. After 0.9 mile turn left at a signed junction on a steep, switchbacking path to the arid cliffs of the bluff. A confusion of paths split off amid juniper, sagebrush, and rock outcrops. Pick your own viewpoint. All of them

36

Hobart Bluff's view. Below: The Pacific Crest Trail on Soda Mountain.

look out across Emigrant Lake's valley to snowy Mt. Ashland.

For the longer hike to Soda Mountain, set out from the trailhead in the other direction, on the Pacific Crest Trail under the powerlines. This route climbs a meadowed slope of June wildflowers: purple larkspur, red paintbrush, pink onion, and yellow composites. When the trail levels off in a grand fir forest after 1.1 mile, watch for a rock cairn marking a side trail that switchbacks up to the left. This unmaintained path climbs past two telephone poles for 0.2 mile to a dirt road. Turn right on the steep road 0.8 mile to Soda Mountain's summit.

The 1933-vintage fire lookout tower atop the peak is now staffed only by a robotic camera. To the south, snowy Mt. Shasta looms above the Klamath River canyon. To return on a loop, follow the lookout's service road (which is closed to unauthorized vehicles) downhill 1.5 miles. Then turn left on gravel Soda Mountain Road 0.4 mile back to your car.

Other Options—Two other bluffs with viewpoints are nearby. To find Little Pilot Rock, follow the PCT south exactly 1 mile past the Soda Mountain cutoff. At a wooded crest, look sharp for the only grassy slope on the right-hand side of the trail that leads *uphill*. Bushwhack up this meadow 0.2 mile to the viewpoint cliff *(GPS location 42.0639 -122.4968)*.

Boccard Point is a further viewpoint, requiring a 10-mile round trip hike with 1200 feet of elevation gain. To find it, continue on the PCT past Little Pilot Rock 0.8 mile down to a pass where half a dozen trails and roads connect. Turn left on the second abandoned dirt road to the left, where boulders block vehicle access to the Wilderness. The correct road goes level to the left for 50 feet, crosses a cattle guard, and then forks. Take the uphill fork to the left for 1.8 miles to its end. Then take a faint trail to the right along a ridgecrest 0.3 mile to Boccard Point *(GPS 42.0491 -122.4829)*, a windswept crag with junipers and stonecrop, overlooking Mt. Shasta.

Hike 5
Pilot Rock

Pioneers once looked to Pilot Rock to find the easiest pass across the Siskiyous from Oregon to California's gold fields.

Moderate (to Pilot Rock)
2.8 miles round trip
1010 feet elevation gain
Open late May through November

Easy (to Rhyolite Ridge)
3.2-mile loop
350 feet elevation gain

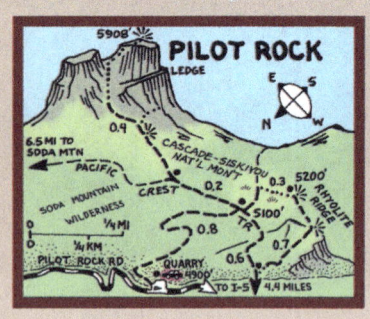

Today Interstate 5 misses this mountaintop Gibraltar by a few miles, but the landmark's sweeping viewpoints and columnar basalt cliffs are just a short hike away in the Soda Mountain Wilderness. The final pitch to the summit of Pilot Rock involves a frighteningly steep scramble. For an easier viewpoint loop, hike to nearby Rhyolite Ridge instead.

Geologically, Pilot Rock is a remnant of a 30-million-year-old lava flow. Whenever basalt lava cools slowly enough, it fractures into hexagonal pillars perpendicular to the cooling surface. The sheer cliffs on Pilot Rock's south and west faces are entirely composed of these 6-sided stone columns. It's a popular practice spot for serious rock climbers.

The area also has a history as a wild hideout. Oregon's last grizzly bear, Old Reelfoot, was felled near the base of Pilot Rock in 1891. In 1923, after the D'Autremont brothers killed three men in a bungled train robbery at the end of the Siskiyou tunnel, they camped under a fallen log near Pilot Rock, eluding a four-continent manhunt.

Pilot Rock from the PCT.

Getting There — From Interstate 5, take Mt. Ashland exit 6 and follow a "Mt. Ashland" pointer onto old Highway 99, paralleling the freeway south. After 0.7 mile go straight under the freeway, following the old highway another 1.2 miles. Beyond the Siskiyou summit 0.4 mile turn left onto Pilot Rock Road 40-2E-33. After 1 mile on this very bumpy one-lane gravel road, ignore a Pacific Crest Trail crossing. After another 1 mile, pull into a large parking area in an old quarry on the right.

The path starts to the left of the restroom and climbs past incense cedars, Jeffrey pines, and blue elderberry bushes. After 0.8 mile you'll reach a pass with the Pacific Crest Trail crossing. Turn left on the PCT for 0.1 mile and then fork to the right on a wide path toward Pilot Rock. Flowers along this rocky, braided route include fuzzy mint, yellow Oregon grape, gooseberry, wild rose, and strawberry.

If you're just out for an easy hike, declare victory at the base of Pilot Rock's cliffs, where the view opens up across Shasta Valley to Mt. Shasta. If you're ready for a scramble, head left up a dusty scree chute along the cliff's base. After another 300 feet, don't follow a ledge angling up to the right—a slippery route that deadends at a cliff. Instead go straight up a very steep chute, using hands and feet to climb past a tricky spot.

At the top the view of Mt. Shasta steals the show. Look to its right to spot Mt. Eddy (with a patch of snow) and the jumbled, distant peaks of the Trinity Alps. Close by to the west is Mt. Ashland, with the white dot of a radar dome on top. If you face north you'll see I-5 snaking between Ashland and Emigrant Lake, while Mt. McLoughlin's cone guards the horizon to the right.

Mt. Shasta from Pilot Rock's base.

If you've climbed Pilot Rock before, or if you'd prefer an easier viewpoint, hike around Rhyolite Ridge instead. From the quarry trailhead, hike 0.8 mile up to the pass. Cross the PCT and continue straight 0.1 mile on a trail downhill. At a rock cairn just before the path reenters the forest, bushwhack up an open meadow slope to the right, directly away from Pilot Rock. After

Columnar basalt on Pilot Rock's summit.

0.2 mile you'll reach a ridgecrest with views of Mt. Shasta and lots of wildflowers

From the ridgecrest, contour to the right on an old roadbed. In another 0.7 mile, when the old road peters out at another open ridge, turn right on the wide, obvious Pacific Crest Trail for 0.6 mile to the pass and the route back to your car.

Pilot Rock from Rhyolite Ridge.

Hike 6

Lithia Park

Before settling down to a play at Ashland's Shakespeare Festival, stretch your legs with a stroll up this woodsy canyon.

Easy
2.8 miles round trip
260 feet elevation gain
Open all year

Boardwalk in the park.

After gold rush miners found gold near Jacksonville in 1851, they found a different treasure here—water. By 1852, Southern Oregon's first lumber mill was using Ashland Creek's power to saw boards for the mines. In 1893, when the Chautauqua movement began bringing lectures and plays to rural areas, the creek's campable woods became a regular stop. In 1908, the architect who designed San Francisco's Golden Gate Park laid out the curving paths, lawns, and gardens of Lithia Park. In 1935, local college professor Angus Bowmer converted an abandoned Chautauqua building into a replica of Shakespeare's open-air Globe theater and launched the tradition of performing plays beside the park.

Getting There— From Medford, take Interstate 5 to Ashland exit 19 and follow signs 2.5 miles into town to a "Lithia Park" sign on the right. If you're driving here from the south, take Ashland exit 14, turn left into town on Ashland Street and Siskiyou Boulevard for 2.7 miles, cross a bridge on the far side of downtown, turn left at a "City Center" pointer, and curve back a block to the Plaza. Dogs are not allowed in Lithia Park.

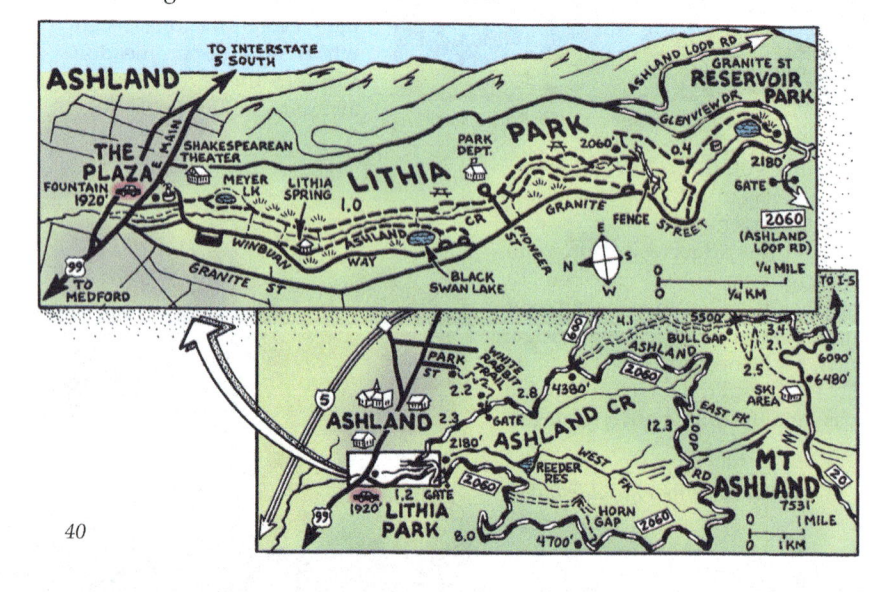

Bridge over Ashland Creek.   Below: Lithia water fountain in The Plaza.

A fountain in the triangular Plaza serves up Lithia Water—a bubbly, bitter combination of sodium, calcium, iron, and bicarbonate piped here from natural springs nearby. After tasting this restorative drink, walk across Winburn Way to Lithia Park (see upper map). Footpaths meander everywhere here, but if you stick to the left-hand bank of Ashland Creek you'll follow increasingly quiet trails for a mile upstream to a fence. To continue, take a small switchback trail uphill to the left. Then turn right on an upper path that leads 0.4 mile up to Granite Street Reservoir—a 200-foot-wide lake with a small sandy beach where swimming is allowed all year, at your own risk.

To explore more of the park on your return trip from the reservoir, retrace your steps 0.2 mile, fork left across the creek, and then follow Lithia Park paths along the left-hand side of the creek where possible.

Other Options— Bicycles aren't allowed in Lithia Park, but one of the grandest mountain bike rides of all time begins here—the 25.4-mile Ashland Loop Road (see lower map). To start from The Plaza, skirt Lithia Park by riding up Winburn Way and then Granite Street for 1.2 miles to the Granite Street Reservoir, where the road turns to gravel. This is also a good place to park a car and start the loop by bike.

From the reservoir, turn left on Glenview Drive for 0.5 mile and then turn right on Ashland Loop Road for 4.7 grueling uphill miles to Four Corners, a 4-way junction with Road 600. From there the loop route turns right, following gravel Road 2060 at a much easier, rolling up-and-down grade for 12.3 miles to Horn Gap, where a thrilling 9.5-mile downhill run shoots you back to The Plaza.

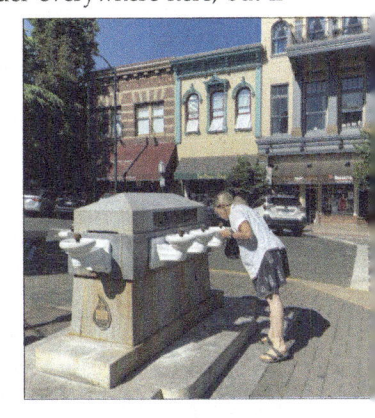

Hike 7
Bandersnatch Trail

"Beware the Jubjub bird, and shun the frumious Bandersnatch," Lewis Carrol wrote in his fantasy poem, "Jabberwocky."

Easy (Bandersnatch Trail)
3.5-mile loop
850 feet elevation gain
Open all year
Use: hikers, horses

Easy (bike route)
3.9-mile loop
850 feet elevation gain
Use: bicycles

Madrone trees along the trail.

Carrol's verse is from his 1872 book, *Through the Looking-Glass and What Alice Found There*. Hikers and mountain bikers may likewise find the hills behind Ashland's Lithia Park fantastical, both for their woodsy charm and because many of the trails are named for Carroll's fantasy inventions.

Local bicyclists pioneered the Alice in Wonderland and BTI trails, which are part of the mountain biking loop recommended here. The Bandersnatch and Red Queen trails, opened more recently, are on a separate loop open only to hikers and equestrians. For a longer adventure, you can connect either loop with the White Rabbit Trail described in Hike #8.

Getting There— From Medford, take Interstate 5 to Ashland exit 19 and follow signs 2.4 miles into town. Just before a bridge over Ashland Creek, turn right on Granite Street for 1.2 steep, uphill miles. After Granite Street turns to gravel, fork left past a swimming reservoir on Glenview Drive for 0.2 mile. Just beyond a sign for the "Waterline Trail" on the right, park in pullouts to the right or left side of the road.

If you're driving here from the south, take Ashland exit 14, turn left into town on Ashland Street and Siskiyou Boulevard for 2.7 miles, cross a bridge on the

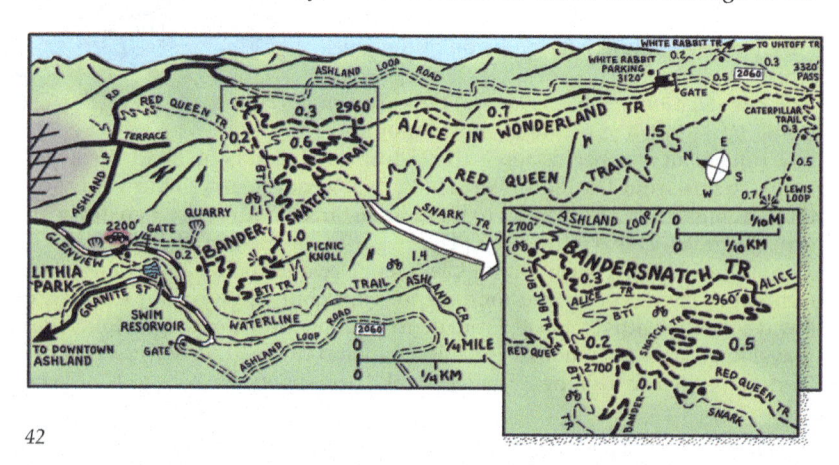

The Bandersnatch Trail.

far side of downtown, turn left at a "City Center" pointer, curve back half a block, turn right on Granite Street 1.2 miles, and fork left on Glenview 0.2 mile.

From your car, walk back to the "Waterline Trail" sign and follow an old gated gravel road through a mixed forest of oak, Douglas fir, madrone, and bigleaf maple. Ignore a driveway and a quarry road to the left. After 0.2 mile you'll reach a junction marked by a post. If you're on a bike, continue straight on the Waterline Trail, a slightly longer route to the top of hill.

If you're on foot (or horseback), however, turn left up some steps to the Bandersnatch Trail. This steepish path switchbacks half a mile up to a picnic knoll with glimpses down Ashland Creek's valley to Ashland. May wildflowers here include fuzzy cat's ears, yellow iris, red paintbrush, and yellow balsamroot.

From the knoll, the Bandersnatch Trail briefly descends, crosses the bike-dominated BTI Trail, and continues half a mile to a junction that marks the start of the loop. Following "Bandersnatch" pointers, veer to the right, but then keep left at the next two junctions. After 0.6 mile you'll crest a ridge to a big X-shaped junction with the Alice in Wonderland Trail. Continue straight on the Bandersnatch Trail, switchbacking down the far side of the ridge 0.3 mile. Just before the Ashland Loop Road, turn left on the Jub Jub Trail. This path contours around the hill 0.2 mile, crossing two bike trails to complete the loop. Then turn right on the Bandersnatch Trail to return 1.2 miles down to your car.

If you're biking, follow the Waterline Trail (which becomes the Snark Trail) for 1.4 miles, turn right on the BTI Trail 300 feet up to the Alice in Wonderland Trail at the crest of the ridge. The Alice path uphill from here crosses some private land. Until easements can be acquired, turn around here and zoom back down the BTI Trail to complete a 3.9-mile loop.

Other Options—For a longer hike, take the Red Queen Trail that opened in 2016. After climbing the Bandersnatch Trail 1.1 mile, keep right on Red Queen for 1.5 miles, traversing in and out along a wooded slope to a pass where you'll meet Road 2060. Turn right on the Caterpillar Trail, switchbacking 0.3 mile uphill, and then turn right on the Lewis Loop, a nearly level, 1.7-mile circuit with views that extend from Mt. McLoughlin to Mt. Ashland. Return as you came.

Hike 8 — White Rabbit Trail

The two paths that climb this scenic, wooded ridge above Ashland cross twice, so hikers can return on a loop.

Moderate
4 miles round trip
1000 feet elevation gain
Open all year
Use: hikers, horses, bicycles

Trail sign.

After two local philanthropists, Vincent Oredson and John Todd, donated ten acres near here in 1983, Ashland businessman Mike Uhtoff led a fundraising campaign with the Southern Oregon Land Conservancy that bought the adjoining 270 acres for Siskiyou Mountain Park in 1992. Today the Mike Uhtoff Trail is for hikers only, while the White Rabbit Trail is also open to mountain bikers and equestrians. At the top of the ridge the trails connect with the Alice in Wonderland Trail (see Hike #7) so it's possible to continue onward toward Lithia Park.

Getting There — From downtown Ashland, take Siskiyou Boulevard south 2.2 miles, turn right on Park Street for 0.6 mile and park just before a "Dead End" sign. The street is extremely steep, so turn your wheels and set your brake.

If you're coming from Interstate 5, take exit 14 (the second Ashland exit), head west into town 0.2 mile on Highway 66, turn left on Tolman Avenue for 0.7 mile, turn right on Siskiyou Boulevard for 0.6 mile, and turn left on Park Street for 0.6 mile.

From your curbside parking spot, walk up the paved street 0.2 mile and veer left onto a wide gravel path, passing a locked brown gate. After 0.4 mile you'll reach a big junction with a mapboard. The White Rabbit Trail for mountain bikers and equestrians is the steep, road-like route up to the right. If you're

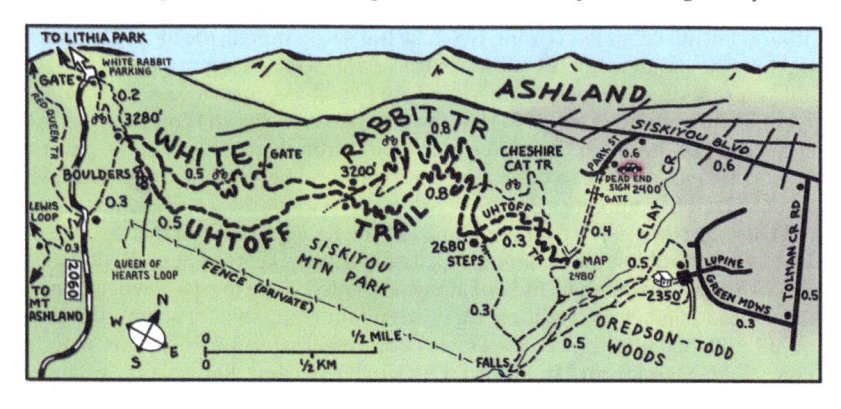

View from the White Rabbit Trail.

hiking, however, walk behind the mapboard to find a smaller, switchbacking path that becomes the Mike Uhtoff Trail. Follow signs to keep on this path as it climbs, crossing the larger White Rabbit Trail twice.

The woods here include oak, madrone, ponderosa pine, poison oak, and Oregon grape. Occasional views open up across Ashland's valley to Grizzly Peak.

After 1.1 mile the Uhtoff Trail veers so close to the White Rabbit Trail that they're connected by a 50-foot link. Avoiding that right-hand spur, and a trail to the left that scrambles up the ridge, continue straight on the Uhtoff Trail, which now traverses a densely wooded slope for half a mile to its end at a switchback of the Queen of Hearts Loop.

For the recommended loop, go left on the Queen of Hearts 0.2 mile, passing a group of ridgecrest boulders, to a big 4-way junction with the White Rabbit Trail. A parking area on Ashland Loop Road 2060 is 0.2 mile ahead, but you might as well turn back here.

For the return trip, why not take the White Rabbit Trail? It is wide and it rollercoasters a bit, but it's no longer than the Uhtoff Trail and has several nice viewpoints. If you're on a bike or a horse, of course, this is the route you've taken all along.

Other Options—For a kid-friendly start to this hike, begin at the Oredson-Todd Trailhead. From exit 14 of Interstate 5, head west into town 0.2 mile on Ashland Hwy 66 and turn left at the first light onto Tolman Creek Road for 1.2 miles. Then turn right on Green Meadows Way for 0.3 mile and take the first left at Lupine Drive to a tight parking area with room for just 4 cars. If you keep to the right at trail junctions from here you'll climb half a mile to the mapboard at the start of the Uhtoff Trail. If you keep left, you amble along Clay Creek half a mile to a small waterfall. See the map for loop options.

Hike 9 Mount Ashland Meadows

There's no handier spot for a stroll through subalpine wildflower meadows than along the Pacific Crest Trail at Mt. Ashland.

Moderate
6.8 miles round trip
600 feet elevation gain
Open mid-June to mid-November
Use: hikers, horses

Trailhead sign.

Starting from a paved road just ten minutes from Interstate 5, this nearly level hike traverses the side of the Siskiyous' tallest peak, with views south to majestic Mt. Shasta. To make the trip even easier, you can shuttle a car or bicycle to Grouse Gap and hike this 3.4-mile section of the PCT one way.

Getting There— Drive I-5 toward the Siskiyou summit and take Mt. Ashland exit 6. Following "Mt. Ashland Ski Area" pointers, parallel the freeway for 0.7 mile and turn right on Mt. Ashland Road 20. After 7.2 miles—just 0.2 mile beyond milepost 7—park at a pullout on the right, identified by a triangular Pacific Crest Trail marker on a tree. Then walk across the road to the trail.

The trail sets off through a forest of grand fir (with flat needles) and Shasta red fir (with upcurved needles). At the half-mile mark the path breaks into the first of five large meadows on the route. In July these slopes blaze with huge blue lupine, fuzy lavender mint, tall purple larkspur, and red paintbrush. By August the show includes yellow daisy-like Bigelow's sneezeweed, petalless brown coneflower, purple aster, white yarrow, and the tiny yellow trumpets of monkeyflower. Look for deer and even black bear in these fields during the early mornings and evenings.

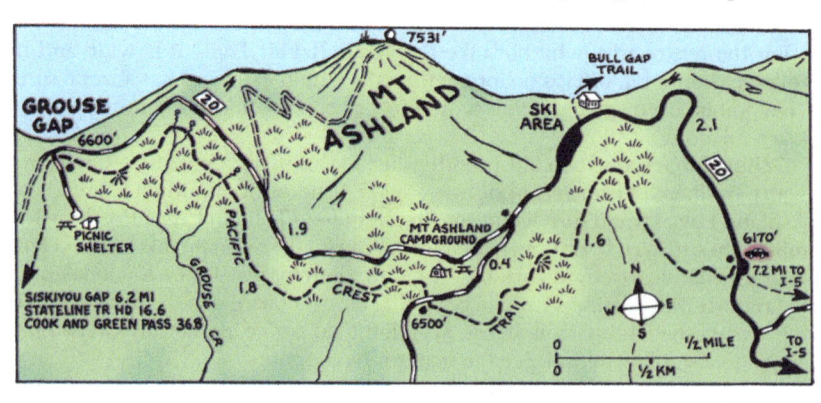

Beyond the second meadow the trail rounds a dry ridge where speckled granite bedrock has been weathered into rounded shapes. Yellow sulphur flower and two kinds of manzanita bushes grow here. After crossing a narrow gravel road at the 1.6-mile mark, you'll get your first views up to Mt. Ashland's summit. A white Doppler radar dome built atop the peak in 1995 resembles an eerie rising moon.

A mile beyond the gravel road the PCT enters a final, broad meadow that wraps around an alpine bowl to Grouse Gap. Joining the flower show here are a few surprising plant visitors from desert country—pungent sagebrush and white-barked quaking aspen. Turn back when the PCT crosses the road to the Grouse Gap picnic shelter. To bring a shuttle car (or bicycle) here from the first trailhead, simply drive 2 miles to Mt. Ashland ski area's huge parking lot and continue straight 2 miles on what becomes a narrow gravel road.

Above and below: The Pacific Crest Trail at Mt. Ashland. Left: Bigelow's sneezeweed in the meadows.

Hike 10

Split Rock

On the rim of the Ashland watershed, this path follows a scenic ridge to Wagner Glade Gap.

Easy (to Split Rock)
2.8 miles round trip
700 feet elevation gain
Open mid-June to mid-November

Moderate (to Wagner Glade Gap)
6 miles round trip
1550 feet elevation gain

Meadow near Split Rock.

Some of the best views are actually near the start of the Split Rock Trail, in the first 0.6 mile to McDonald Peak. For a truly panoramic view, ambitious hikers can continue all the way to Wagner Butte.

Getting There — Drive Interstate 5 south toward the Siskiyou summit and take Mt. Ashland exit 6. Following "Mt. Ashland Ski Area" pointers, parallel the freeway for 0.7 mile and turn right on Mt. Ashland Road 20. After 9 miles you'll reach the Mt. Ashland Ski Area parking lot. At the far end of this long, paved lot, go straight on Road 20, which suddenly narrows to one lane gravel. Continue 2.2 miles to Grouse Gap, avoiding turnoffs for the Mt. Ashland Campground to the left and Mt. Ashland's Summit Road to the right. At Grouse Gap there's a small parking pullout on the right for the Pacific Crest Trail, which touches the road on the left. Ignore all of this, and instead keep right on Road 20 for another 1.3 rough, uphill miles.

Watch your odometer carefully, because the Split Rock Trailhead is easy to miss. Exactly 1.3 mile beyond Grouse Gap, on a sagebrush slope to the right, look for a small wooden "Split Rock Trail" sign *(GPS location 42.076 -122.7483)*. A rough dirt pullout on the right here has room for only three cars — and unfortunately there's no other parking nearby.

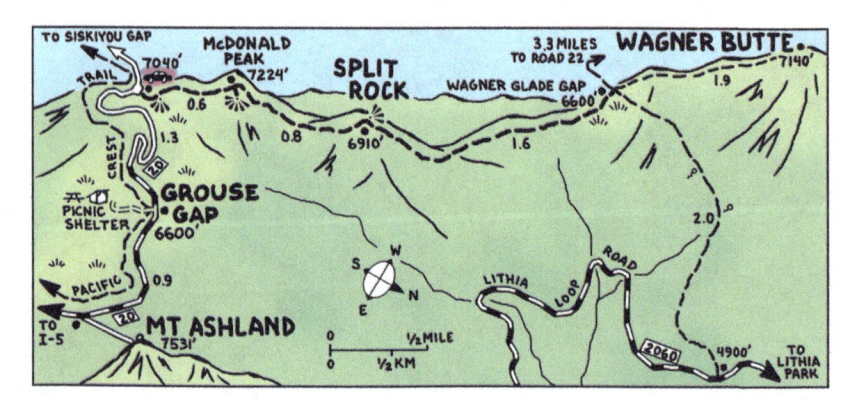

48

Mt. Ashland from the start of the Split Rock Trail.

The trail sets off through the hiker-only McDonald Botanical Area, a meadow of sagebrush and low manzanita. July wildflowers here include scarlet gilia, lupine, yellow buckwheat, and fuzzy blue mint flowers that attract butterflies.

After ambling up and down along a broad ridge for 0.6 mile you'll reach a fork with a "Trail" sign pointing left. Before heeding the sign, go right 50 feet to the summit of McDonald Peak, a white granite outcrop with 360-degree views. The green hill ahead to the north is Wagner Butte. To the east, distant Mt. McLoughlin rises above Ashland's valley. Mt. Ashland is easy to recognize because of its white radar dome. To the south, Mt. Shasta is a white ghost.

If you're hiking with kids, turn back here. Otherwise continue another 0.8 mile to Split Rock, a less panoramic outcrop of big granite boulders. This is a second possible turnaround point, because the trail then plummets 300 feet before continuing along the ridge. Another 1.6 miles on this up-and-down trail brings you to an X-shaped trail junction in Wagner Glade Gap, a sagebrush meadow with lesser views.

Scarlet gilia amid asters.

Other Options — If Wagner Glade Gap seems an unsatisfactory destination, and if you're going strong, continue straight on the well-graded 1.9-mile trail to the summit of Wagner Butte.

Hike 11 — Wagner Butte

The best view of the Ashland area isn't from Mt. Ashland, but rather from this less-known 7140-foot peak nearby.

Difficult
10.4 miles round trip
2200 feet elevation gain
Open mid-June to mid-November
Use: hikers, horses

Wagner Butte from the PCT.

With binoculars, hikers atop Wagner Butte can pick out most of the individual buildings in Ashland, a vertical mile below. The demanding trail to the top offers other rewards as well—old-growth firs, an interesting landslide regrowing with wildflowers, a cold spring, sagebrush meadows, and an unusual quaking aspen grove.

The butte's name recalls Jacob Wagner, an early Talent settler who served in the 1853 Indian War and ran the flour mill at Ashland's Plaza. After a 1910 forest fire burned much of Ashland Creek's canyon and threatened Ashland, the Forest Service agreed to set up a fire lookout atop the butte. Staff made do with an open-air observation post until a cupola-style building could be built in 1923. Winter storms blew parts of the structure off the mountain. The building was finally replaced in 1961, but by then airplanes were taking over fire surveillance. Abandoned after just a few summers, the tower was intentionally burned by smokejumpers in 1972, leaving only foundation piers, melted glass, an iron railing, and the extraordinary view.

Getting There— From Interstate 5 south of Medford, take Talent exit 21, head west on Valley View Road for 0.4 mile, turn left on S. Pacific Highway for 0.3 mile, turn right on Rapp Road for 0.9 mile to the second stop sign, and continue straight on Wagner Creek Road. After 4.6 miles this road crosses a bridge and narrows to one lane. Keeping left at forks after this point, continue

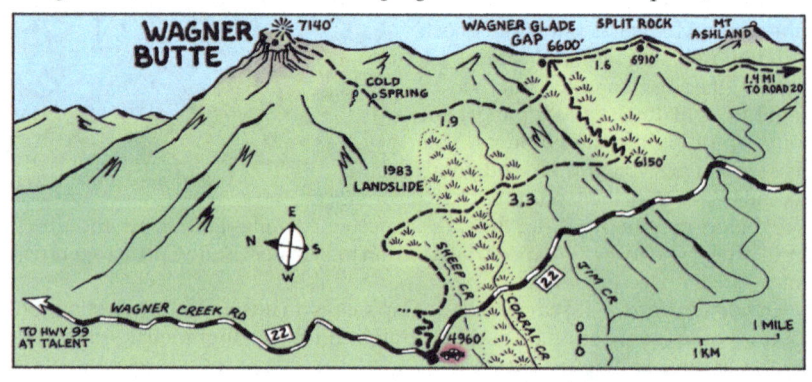

The view north from the foundations of Wagner Butte's burned lookout tower.

uphill 3.9 paved miles to Wagner Gap, and another 2 miles on good gravel to the trailhead, marked only by a post on the left and a large parking area amid big pine trees on the right.

The trail starts with a dozen steep little switchbacks up to an old roadbed amid ponderosa pines with beargrass clumps, orange paintbrush, and speckled granite rocks. Then the path climbs more gently, traversing old Douglas fir woods with occasional meadowed slopes. The largest of these meadows is the Sheep Creek Slide, where a May 1983 thundershower sent 400,000 tons of soil, trees, and granite from Wagner Butte sliding 4 miles to the Little Applegate River. The Forest Service has since seeded the slide with grass and opened

Wagner Glade Gap.

it to cattle grazing, but a wealth of native flowers also thrive here. In summer look for blue lupine, petalless brown coneflower, bulbous yellow sneezeweed, and sweet-smelling mint.

At the 2.4-mile mark the trail suddenly begins switchbacking up a steep sagebrush meadow for 0.9 mile to Wagner Glade Gap, where a trail joins from Split Rock on the right. Then the path ambles along for the final 1.9 miles, passing wind-gnarled mountain mahogany, white-barked quaking aspen, and a cold, piped spring before clambering up a stack of car-sized granite boulders to the summit. From here, the strip of urban development between Medford and Ashland looks like white confetti strewn along Interstate 5, with the dark squares of orchards on either hand. To the right stretch the forests of the Ashland's watershed valley, topped by Mt. Ashland and its white Doppler radar dome. Farther to the right look for snowy Mt. Shasta, the distant Marble Mountains, Red Buttes, flat-topped Preston Peak, and broad Grayback Mountain.

Hike 12

Jack-Ash Trail

What do you name a trail linking Jacksonville with Ashland? The Jack-Ash Trail, of course.

Easy
3-mile loop
500 feet elevation gain
Open April to December
Use: hikers, horses, bicycles

Phlox on Anderson Butte.

The Jack-Ash Trail is the brainchild of the Siskiyou Upland Trails Association, a Jacksonville group of equestrians, hikers, and mountain bikers. A portion of the proposed 40-mile route has already been opened across Anderson Butte, with meadow slopes full of wildflowers from late April to mid-June. An easy loop takes you to a viewpoint atop Anderson Butte's old lookout site.

Getting There — From Interstate 5, take South Medford exit 27, follow signs west toward Highway 99 for half a mile to a light, turn left on South Pacific Highway for 1.2 miles to the third light, and turn right on South Stage Road for 3.1 miles to a T-shaped junction. Turn left on Griffin Creek Road and drive 2.2 miles to a sharp left turn with a "Jack-Ash Trail" pointer. After turning left, stay on Griffin Creek Road for another 1.9 miles. When Griffin Creek Road turns sharply left again and becomes gravel, go straight to stay uphill on the main paved road. Continue on what is now one-lane Anderson Butte Road for 3.8 miles to Griffin Gap, a saddle with a 4-way road junction where pavement ends.

The Griffin Gap Trailhead of the Jack-Ash Trail is here, but this part of the path goes downhill through woods. For a more interesting hike, turn sharply left and follow the gravel road (with some potholes and washboard) for 3.4 miles, keeping left at junctions, to a dirt parking pullout on the right with a large "Anderson

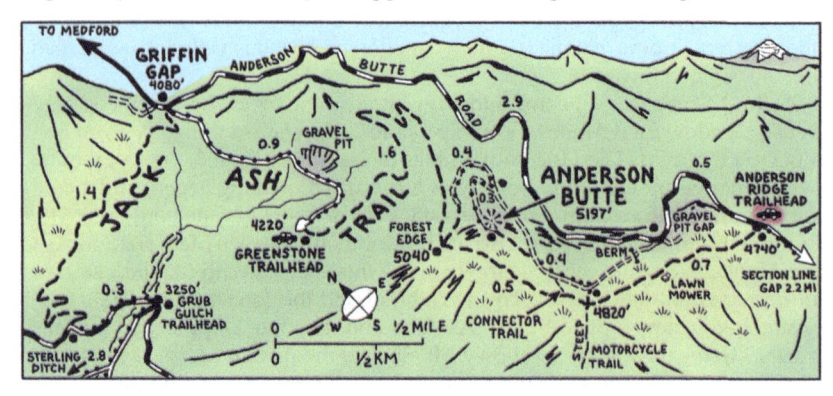

52

The Jack-Ash Trail.

Ridge Trailhead" sign and a hiker registration box *(GPS 42.1926 -122.8848).*

The nearly level trail sets out across a meadowed slope that faces south, so it's dry enough to resemble the high desert, with sagebrush and juniper. But you will also see wildflowers—purple larkspur, red fritillaries, and pink plectritis.

The trail weaves around rock outcrops of red peridotite and green serpentine, nutrient-poor minerals that were churned up from the Earth's mantle when the Klamath/Siskiyou mountains collided with the North American continent.

At the 0.7-mile mark you'll cross a motorcycle trail, marked with posts that warn about proper trail usage. Here you'll also see the first Jeffrey pines of the hike and enter a cooler slope with miners lettuce and bleeding hearts.

Another half mile along the Jack-Ash Trail takes you to a ridge-end corner where the trail suddenly enters a dense Douglas fir forest. For the loop, turn uphill on a smaller, unmarked trail that leads to an old roadbed circling Anderson Butte. Follow this roadbed 0.4 mile, turn sharply right on another old road uphill, and follow it 0.3 mile to a flat spot at road's end beside the summit.

The lookout tower that once stood atop Anderson Butte is gone, but eight concrete foundation piers remain, and so does the view. To continue the loop, walk straight from road's end onto a motorcycle path that continues downhill along a ridge for 0.2 mile to the old, abandoned lookout road. Turn right on the roadbed, watching for a faint connector trail down to the right that leads just 300 feet to rejoin the Jack-Ash Trail.

If you miss that connector trail to the right, don't panic. After 0.2 mile the old roadbed curves sharply left into the open. Just 50 feet beyond this corner a motorcycle path dives steeply down to the right through a patch of head-high serviceberry bushes. This connector is much steeper, with slippery pebbles, but it's only 200 feet to the Jack-Ash Trail. Turn left to return to your car.

Other Options—The Jack-Ash Trail makes possible a 38-mile loop for equestrians or mountain bikers, connecting with either end of the Sterling Ditch Trail (see Hike #14).

Hike 13 East Applegate Ridge

A new link in the proposed trail between Ashland and Grants Pass has wildflower slopes with views to the snowy Siskiyous.

Easy (to crest viewpoint)
2.4 miles round trip
150 feet elevation gain
Open all year,
Use: hikers, horses, bicycles

Easy (entire trail, with shuttle)
5 miles one way
150 feet elevation gain

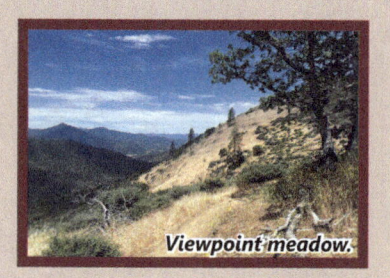

Viewpoint meadow.

For a quick trip, turn back at the highest point of the trail, where there's a view across the fields of Ruch to the Applegate Valley. Want to see more? Because the rest of the path is downhill, losing 1320 feet of elevation, it's easiest if you can arrange a short car shuttle to the far trailhead.

Getting There— Drive Interstate 5 to North Medford exit #30 and head west on Highway 238 for 5.6 miles to Jacksonville. At a T-shaped junction in downtown, turn right to continue on Highway 238. At a pass after another 2.9 miles, turn left on Cady Road for 0.5 mile. Then turn right on Sterling Creek Road for 4.1 miles. Finally turn right on one-lane gravel BLM Road 38-2-29.1 for 0.6 mile to its end at a large gravel parking lot with a restroom. Ignore a "Route End" post and instead start at a "Trail" post by the parking lot entrance.

The path climbs gradually through a mixed forest of Douglas fir, madrone, pine, and scrub oak. The route is so popular with dogwalkers that leashes are advised. Stay on the trail to avoid poison oak.

Meadow openings and views increase on the way to the highest point of the trail, a viewpoint at the 1.2-mile mark. Wildflowers peak in late April. Expect the blooms of sunflower-like mules ears, purple ookow, and pink farewell-to-spring. The view includes a butte to the south where hang gliders launch. To

View of Ruch from the trail.   Below: Ookow bloom.

the southwest, Tallowbox Mountain (Hike #18) is a bare knoll, with snowy Grayback Mountain peering over its shoulder on the horizon.

If you continue past this possible turnaround point 0.9 mile you'll reach a bench at another ridge-end meadow. The view here is even broader, encompassing the entire Siskiyou crest from Mt. Ashland (on the left) to Red Buttes. Beyond the bench the trail descends through woods and small meadow openings for 2 miles to the western trailhead.

To shuttle a car here from the first trailhead, drive back to Sterling Creek Road, follow it left 4.1 miles to Cady Road, turn left for half a mile to Highway 238, and turn left toward Ruch for 2.3 miles. At an "East Applegate Ridge Trail" sign (just before milepost 28) turn left into a large gravel parking lot with a picnic table but no shade. The trail begins at a locked green gate, following an old road uphill for 0.7 mile before narrowing to a single-track path.

The East Applegate Ridge Trail is a central link in the proposed Siskiyou Ridge Trail, a route that would eventually connect Cathedral Hills Park in Grants Pass with Jacksonville and Ashland. For a map of the entire route, or to volunteer for trail work, see *applegatetrails.org*.

Hike 14
Sterling Ditch Tunnel

Three years after the 1851 discovery of gold at Jacksonville, miners struck paydirt in Sterling Creek.

Easy
4.8-mile loop
550 feet elevation gain
Open all year
Use: hikers, horses, bicycles

Poison oak.

After the easy ore was panned out of Sterling Creek, quite a bit of gold dust remained in the ancient river gravels stranded on dry slopes high above the stream. But how could miners get water up there to wash the gold loose?

That question launched one of Southern Oregon's most remarkable engineering projects—a 26.5-mile ditch carrying water from the Little Applegate River to the Sterling Creek hills. Hand-dug by nearly 400 Chinese laborers in 1877, the 3-foot-deep ditch remained in use until the 1930s.

Today the Sterling Mine Ditch lives on as a 23.2-mile recreation trail winding through the oak grasslands and pine forests of the upper Applegate country. While much of this route is best appreciated from the saddle of a mountain bike or a horse, hikers can sample the trail's highlights on an easy, 4.8-mile loop to an explorable 100-foot tunnel where the ditch ducks through a ridge.

Clarkia.

Getting There— From Medford, follow signs west to Jacksonville and continue straight on Highway 238 for 8 miles to the settlement of Ruch. (If you're coming from Grants Pass, follow signs south to Murphy and continue straight on Highway 238 to Ruch, between mileposts 25 and 26.)

In Ruch, turn south toward the Upper Applegate area for 2.9 miles. Then turn left on Little Applegate Road for 9.7 miles to the Tunnel Ridge Trailhead parking pullout on the right. The trail climbs through oak woodlands mixed with Douglas fir, ponderosa pine, and Douglas maples. Expect wildflowers in May and June: pink clarkia, tall blue ookow, lilac-like deerbrush, and the pinkish, ball-shaped blooms of wild onion. Watch out for poison oak's triple leaflets. After 1 mile the path reaches the old ditch at the tunnel. Just 4 feet high, the tunnel is tight for adults but easy enough for children to hike through.

To continue the loop, walk left along the dry ditch's rim for 2.2 miles, passing huge madrone trees and a collapsed trestle along the way. Then turn left at a trail sign on a ridge end, take a 1-mile path down Bear Gulch to Little Applegate Road, and follow this gravel road left for 0.6 mile to your car.

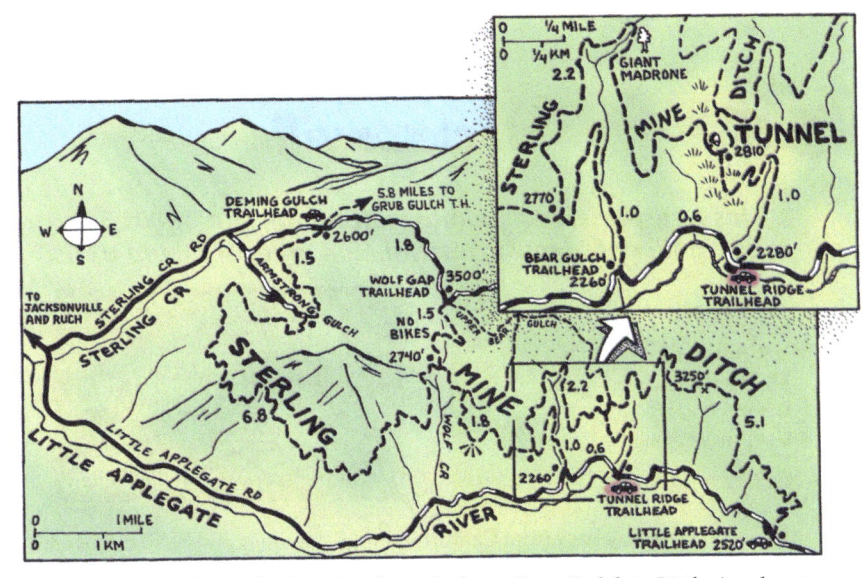

Other Options—If you'd like to see more of the 23.2-mile Sterling Mine Ditch Trail, you can start at any of six different trailheads (see map). For an 11.6-mile loop that doesn't require a car shuttle, begin at Wolf Gap. From there, a scenic spur trail (closed to bikes) descends 1.5 miles to the ditch. Turn right for 8.3 miles to the Deming Gulch Trailhead and walk up the road 1.8 miles to complete the loop. To find the Wolf Gap Trailhead, drive Little Applegate Road to milepost 3, turn north on paved Sterling Creek Road for 2.1 miles, turn right on gravel Armstrong Gulch Road 39-2-17 for 0.3 mile, and fork left on Deming Gulch Road for 2.5 miles.

An even grander 38-mile loop has been developed by the Siskiyou Upland Trails Association. The "Jack-Ash Trail" is planned to eventually link Jacksonville with Ashland, but a completed segment connects the trailheads at either end of the Sterling Mine Ditch Trail. The loop uses 9.2 miles of quiet backroads and 4.2 miles of new trail to traverse Anderson Butte's ridge, northeast of the ditch trail. See Hike #12 and *sutaoregon.org* for details.

Right: giant madrone on the ditch.

57

Hike 15
Jacksonville

This well-preserved boomtown from the mid-1800s has shops, galleries, a music festival, and miles of hiking trails.

Easy
3.3-mile loop
350 feet elevation gain
Open all year
Use: hikers, bicycles

Jacksonville Trolley.

Miners on their way back from California's more famous Gold Rush discovered gold here in Rich Gulch in 1852. The tent-and-plank town that sprang up was briefly Oregon's largest. After the easy gold was panned out, giant hydraulic hoses washed away acres of land in search of gold dust. When the new railroad line through Southern Oregon bypassed Jacksonville in favor of Medford in 1886, the city slipped into a kind of suspended animation, lacking the money to remodel or even to tear down buildings. The entire city was declared a National Historic Landmark in 1966, and a reawakening began.

Getting There — Start at an 1891 railroad depot converted to a visitor center on Oregon and C streets. If you're coming from Interstate 5, take Medford exit 30 and follow signs 7 miles to Jacksonville on Highway 238. At a "Britt Parking" sign opposite Jacksonville's City Hall, turn right on C Street for four blocks to its end at the visitor center.

Start at the far end of the parking lot, where a sign announces the entrance to Jacksonville Woodlands Park. Cross the highway on a crosswalk and climb a set of stairs into the Britt Gardens. Stone walls here mark the site of the home of Peter Britt, a Swiss-born miner, painter, vintner, and photographer whose acclaimed pictures documented early Southern Oregon.

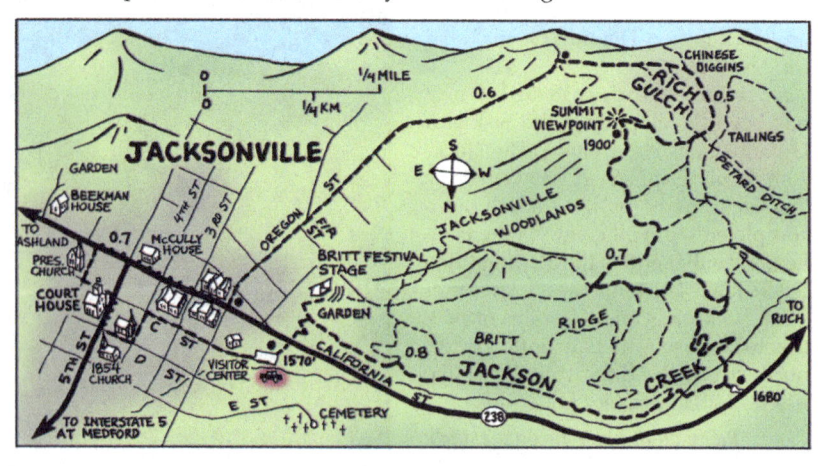

California Street in Jacksonville.

    A walkway to the left leads to the amphitheater where the Britt Festival's open-air concerts are held on summer evenings. For the loop hike, however, turn right instead, following a pointer for the Sara Zigler Interpretive Trail. After just 150 feet you'll pass a 4-foot-diameter sequoia planted by Peter Britt in 1862 on the day his son Emil was born. Then the path enters a forest of Douglas fir, madrone, white oak, and ponderosa pine.

    After half a mile, turn right across a footbridge over Jackson Creek, continue upstream to a parking area, and turn left across another footbridge. Then follow signs for "Rich Gulch" and "Panoramic Viewpoint," taking a left turn followed by two right turns and two lefts, to find a knolltop bench overlooking the town and Mt. McLoughlin.

View from Jacksonville Woods.

    After admiring the view, continue 300 feet to a trail junction, turn right, and then keep straight at all junctions to descend through Rich Gulch. Trailside signs describe the flumes and giant hydraulic hoses that washed gold from this valley, leaving cobble tailings.

    When you reach paved Oregon Street, turn left for 0.6 mile to the town's historic center, with shops, galleries, and the restored 1856 Bella Union Saloon. To continue the walking tour, turn right along California Street four blocks, passing the clapboard 1860 McCully House. Turn left at the Victorian Gothic 1881 Presbyterian Church on Sixth Street to find the 1883 county courthouse (now the city hall). Then zigzag to Fifth and D Streets to see two rival Protestant and Catholic churches from the 1850s before returning along C Street to your car.

Grants Pass Area

Sunset fog in the Siskiyou Mountains.
Below: Mt. Elijah (Hike #23).

The Rogue River near Grave Creek (Hike #26).
Below: Indian Warrior.

Left: Madrone tree bark.
Below: The Rogue River at Grants Pass.

Hike 16 Grants Pass Nature Trails

These four easy loop trails are close enough together that you can do several in one day.

Easy (Dollar Mountain)
3.1-mile loop
830 feet elevation gain
Open all year

Easy (Cathedral Hills)
3.4-mile loop
300 feet elevation gain

Easy (Limpy Creek)
1-mile loop
120 feet elevation gain

Easy (Waters Creek)
3.4-mile loop
400 feet elevation gain

Waters Creek Trail.

Dollar Mountain is the closest to downtown Grants Pass, the steepest, and the least kid-friendly. On the south edge of town, the Cathedral Hills loop is stunning when the Indian warrior wildflowers bloom in spring. Limpy Creek has a little waterfall that's a fine goal for kids. The Waters Creek loop extends from a meadow into a canyon of big Douglas fir trees.

Getting There — To find the Dollar Mountain trailhead from Interstate 5, take the north Grants Pass exit #58, follow Sixth Street into town 1.5 miles, turn right on A Street for a block, jog left a block to circumvent the courthouse, and take B Street for 1.1 miles. Sticking to the largest street,

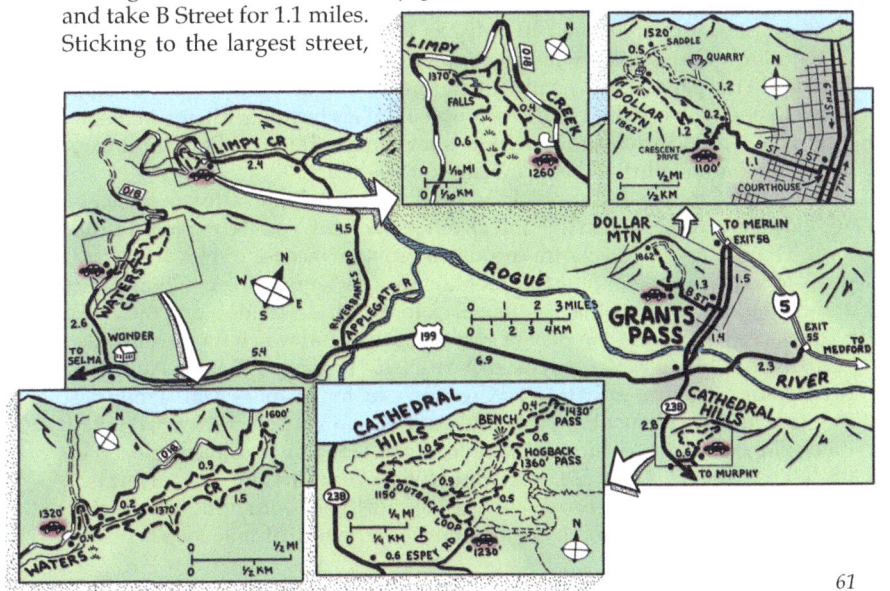

Wildflowers at Cathedral Hills.

avoid a dead end to the left and later curve left on Crescent Drive for 0.2 mile to a signed parking pullout on the left.

The Dollar Mountain trail begins on the uphill side of the street and climbs through a black oak scrubland with the blooms of purple vetch and fuzzy cats ears in early summer. Beware of three-leaved poison oak beside the trail. After 1.2 miles you'll reach a great viewpoint, just before trail's end at a fenced communication tower on Dollar Mountain's summit. To return on a loop, continue on a service road down from the summit half a mile to a saddle. Fork right and continue downhill on the road 1.2 miles to Crescent Drive, where you'll have walk up to the right 0.2 mile to your car.

To find the easier nature trails at Cathedral Hills, take Sixth Street south from downtown across the river and veer onto Highway 238 toward Murphy for 2.8 miles. At a "Cathedral Hills" sign, turn left on Espey Road for 0.3 mile and fork left to stay on Espey Road another 0.3 mile to its end at a turnaround—the hub for a 10-mile network of trails. This area also has the state's largest knobcone pine (117 feet) and the largest whiteleaf manzanita (25 feet). The slopes here blaze with wildflowers from April to June. Poison oak is common too, so stay on the trail. From the parking area, walk past the outhouse 50 feet and fork to the right to set out on a 3.4-mile tour, following "Outback Loop" signs at junctions. The route climbs 1.1 mile to a pass and turns left along a ridge 0.4 mile to a bench with a view of Grants Pass. Continue 1.9 miles to complete the Outback Loop back to your car.

To find the Limpy Creek trailhead from Grants Pass, follow signs for Crescent City on Highway 199 for 10 miles. At the far side of the Applegate River bridge, at milepost 7, turn right onto Riverbanks Road. After 4.5 miles, turn left on paved Limpy Creek Road (which becomes Road 018) for 2.4 miles to the Limpy Botanical Trail parking area on the left. Limpy was the derogatory "white" name given to one of two Indian brothers whose families lived near here. Archeologists in 1996 found arrowheads, middens, and notched stone fishing net sinkers, revealing that the site had been a village for 600 years.

The Limpy Creek Trail starts beside an outhouse and climbs 50 feet to a junction at a kiosk. If you keep left at this and all other junctions, you'll complete a 1-mile loop. The route switchbacks up through a grove of incense cedars and Jeffrey pines to a dry hillside of bluish serpentine rock. After 0.6 mile the loop passes an 8-foot waterfall. The final 0.4 mile back to the car descends along the creek, with places where kids can play at gravel beaches, but watch for poison oak.

To find the hike at Waters Creek, drive back to Highway 199 at the Applegate River bridge and turn right toward Crescent City for 5.4 miles. Half a mile past the store in the settlement of Wonder, turn right on Waters Creek Road for 1.9 miles of pavement and another 0.7 mile of one-lane gravel to the trailhead on the left *(GPS 42.3904 -123.5547)*. The trail follows the creek up to a culvert by a pond and then ambles through a white oak grassland with mint, balsamroot, and bachelor buttons. Keep left at junctions for the full 3.4-mile loop.

Hike 17   Enchanted Forest

An easy trail through these enchanted woods leads to a creekside memorial. A steeper climb visits a viewpoint.

Easy (to Felton memorial)
4.4 miles round trip
400 feet elevation gain
Open all year
Use: hikers, horses, bicycles

Moderate (to saddle viewpoint)
3.8 miles round trip
1000 feet elevation gain

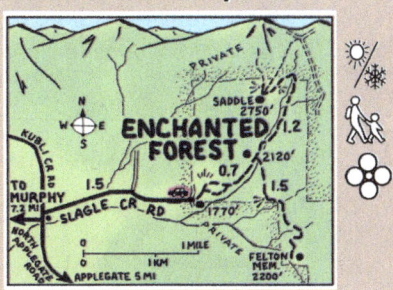

After the federal government granted a railroad company a checkerboard of land to build track from California to Oregon in the late 1800s, this square mile of low-elevation forest became a forgotten valley, almost entirely trapped by private clearcuts and ranches. But one small route of public access remained. Now this trailhead is your gateway to the Enchanted Forest.

Getting There — From Interstate 5, take Grants Pass exit #55, drive Highway 199 through town 2 miles, and follow signs onto Highway 238 for 6.3 miles to Murphy. Just before downtown Murphy, turn left on North Applegate Road toward Missouri Flat. At a T-shaped junction after 7.2 miles, turn briefly left on Kubli Creek Road and then promptly turn right on paved Slagle Creek Road for 1.5 miles to its end, where a green metal gate marks the start of the trail.

Meadow on the trail.

There are only three parking spaces here, and you can't block the private gravel driveways to the left or right, so expect to drive back 0.1 mile, where you can park along the south shoulder of Slagle Creek Road.

From the gate the trail ambles through mixed woods of ponderosa pine, Douglas fir, and madrone, with wildflowers in April and May. After 0.1 mile the path forks in a meadow. Either route works. The paths rejoin in 0.2 mile and pass an old homestead site with a shot-up 1950s pickup. Then you enter shady maple woods along a creek.

At the 0.7-mile mark you'll reach a junction and face a decision. For an easier hike, turn right on the Felton Trail, which contours 1.5 miles, passing some viewpoints among the madrones, to trail's end at a granite slab honoring three men who died here in a helicopter crash in 1993. The glen has a small creek and a campsite where you can eat lunch, but the trails beyond this are all private, so you really do have to turn back.

If you take the other path at the junction, you'll continue up the Enchanted Forest Trail 0.9 mile to the head of a lovely little creek. Then the path switchbacks left and climbs steeply 0.3 mile to a forested saddle with a view.

Hike 18 Tallowbox Mountain

Hike to views atop this Applegate Valley peak on ancient roadbeds reopened as pleasant hiking trails n 2024.

Moderate (from upper trailhead)
3 miles round trip
930 feet elevation gain
Open all year
Use: hikers, horses, bicycles

Difficult (from lower trailhead)
7 miles round trip
2390 feet elevation gain

Cobwebby thistles.

You can hike up Tallowbox Mountain two different ways—either through meadows from an upper trailhead or on a more strenuous route that climbs from a lower trailhead at Ladybug Gulch. Either way, for the final half mile you'll follow a gated road up to a panoramic view beside the summit's 100-foot telecommunication tower.

Getting There— Start by driving Highway 238 south of Jacksonville (or east of Murphy). To find the upper trailhead, turn off Highway 238 a mile west of the community of Ruch—between mileposts 24 and 25, turn south on Hamilton Road. After one mile, turn right across a one-lane concrete bridge onto Cantrall Road. Ignore a campground to the left. Continue on the one-lane road for 5.1 miles of pavement and another 1.9 miles of gravel to a saddle with a small parking area to the left and a small "Tallowbox Trail" sign.

From this upper trailhead, the path ambles along a slope through sparse woods of Douglas firs and ponderosa pines. The spiny-looking shrub here is buckbrush. Meadow openings along the way have views south to distant snowy Red Buttes.

From April to June the meadows are spangled with flowers—the big red blooms of cobwebby thistle, pink 4-petaled farewell-to-spring, tall blue dicks, blue lupine, and orange poppies.

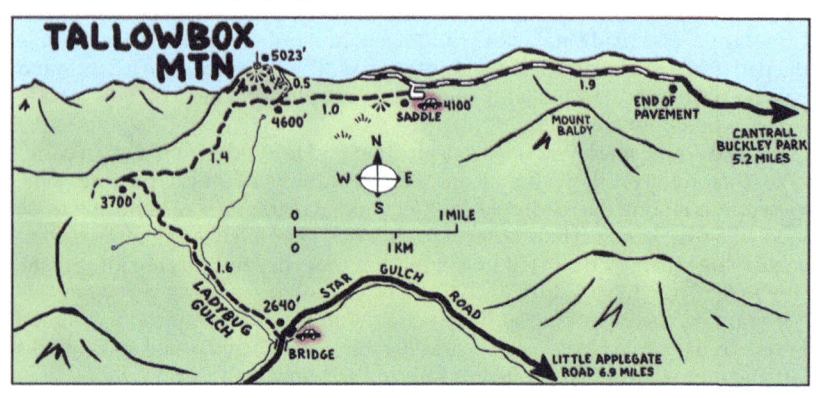

After a mile you'll reach a junction with an old road. Turn uphill to the right on this track. Then keep left at junctions to climb past a locked gate on a rough service road to the summit tower. The white blooms on foot-tall stalks here are death camas, a poisonous relative of edible blue camas. The summit's view to the east extends past the fields at Ruch and a faint stripe of Medford to distant Mt. McLoughlin and Crater Lake's rim.

If this hike seemed too easy, or if you've done it before, start at the lower trailhead instead. To find it, drive Highway 238 to the community of Ruch, between mileposts 25 and 26. Next to Ramsay Realty, turn south on Upper Applegate Road. After 6.4 miles look sharp for Star Goulch Road on the right. This turnoff is easy to miss; if you reach the Star Ranger Station you've gone 0.2 mile too far. Drive one-lane paved Star Gulch Road for 5.9 miles to a small "Tallowbox Trail" sign bolted to a tree on the right, 50 feet before the paved road crosses a concrete bridge. Park at a small pullout before the sign *(GPS location 42.1723 -123.144)*.

Lupines bloom along the trail.

The trail begins as a grassy old roadbed up Ladybug Gulch, a valley with a small creek shaded by Douglas maples. The route gains nearly 2000 feet in 3 miles to the road junction described above. Then you keep left on roads for half a mile to the summit.

Mount Baldy from a meadow near the upper trailhead.

Hike 19 — Collings Mountain

Hikers in this remote part of the Siskiyou Range have been reporting sightings of Bigfoot since 1895.

Easy (to Bigfoot trap)
1.2 miles round trip
200 feet elevation gain
Open all year
Use: hikers, horses, bicycles

Moderate (to Watkins Campground)
6.9 miles one way
1700 feet elevation gain
Open except in winter storms

Bigfoot trap.

In 1973, when a private research group resolved to catch the mythic apeman outright, they built their trap here. Today an easy half-mile trail from Applegate Lake leads to the abandoned contraption. If you believe more in exercise than in Sasquatch, consider following the woodsy trail another 6.3 miles, across Collings Mountain to the far end of Applegate Lake's reservoir.

Getting There— From Medford, follow signs west to Jacksonville and continue straight on Highway 238 for 8 miles to the settlement of Ruch. (From Grants Pass, follow signs south to Murphy and continue straight on Highway 238 to Ruch, between mileposts 25 and 26.) In Ruch, turn south toward the Upper Applegate area for 15.9 miles. When you've driven 1 mile past Applegate Dam turn left into the Hart-Tish Recreation Area. Expect a $5 day-use fee.

Park in the picnic area parking lot on the right, walk to a large "Applegate Lake" sign at the upper end of the lot, and veer left on a level trail into the woods. After 0.1 mile, cross the highway to find a path that switchbacks down into a gulch and follows a mossy creek up through a forest of Douglas fir, white pine, madrone, and bigleaf maple. Keep an eye out for poison oak.

After 0.6 mile the path splits around the dilapidated caretaker's cabin, a shake-sided 9-by-12-foot shack. From here, a spur trail to the left climbs to the Bigfoot trap, a formidable 10-foot-tall cell with thick walls and a guillotine-like steel door. Poison oak is thick here.

If you decide to continue, return to the main trail and follow it up the canyon 0.3 mile to a prospector's adit—a short tunnel built to check for ore. Beyond this the trail climbs steeply up a hillside of scrub oak and madrone, with glimpses out to Applegate Lake. Then the path follows a broad ridge 2 miles before switchbacking past a grassy opening that is the summit of Collings Mountain. Although this mountaintop lacks views, the open woods host a surprising variety of June wildflowers: beargrass plumes, fuzzy white lupine, trumpet-shaped purple penstemon, tall blue ookow, pink clarkia, and white iris.

Glimpse of Applegate Lake from Collings Mountain.

Beyond the summit, the trail descends 2.9 miles through the woods before crossing the paved road to the Watkins Campground parking area. Ideally you'll have left a shuttle car or bicycle here for a quick ride back to the starting trailhead. If not, walk to the far left end of the parking lot and take the Da-Ku-Be-Te-De Trail, a path that parallels the reservoir's shore (and the road) for 3.4 miles back to your car.

67

Hike 20
Red Buttes

Lakes are rare in the Siskiyous, but the Pacific Crest Trail passes near two as it skirts Red Buttes.

Moderate (to Lilypad Lake)
8.2 miles round trip
1440 feet elevation gain
Open June to mid-November
Use: hikers, horses

Red Buttes from the PCT.

This rocky, double-topped mountain is the landmark of the Red Buttes Wilderness. The buttes are made of peridotite, a red, iron-rich rock created when seafloor basalt is baked inside the earth. The 200 million-year-old rock tells a lot about the history of this range. The Siskiyous formed as the North American continent crunched westward over the Pacific plate, scraping off seafloor sediments and volcanic island chains like cake batter on a spatula.

Patches of white marble on the side of Red Buttes are the remains of seashells, cooked and contorted by pressure. Outcrops of greasy-looking, greenish-black serpentine rock along the Pacific Crest Trail are the lubricant that formed between the sliding plates of continent and seafloor. An old road paralleling the PCT was built by miners searching for gold, chromium, and other heavy metals churned up by the titanic collision of crustal plates.

The trailhead and the first 2 miles of trail are still recovering from a 2017 fire.

Getting There — From Medford, follow signs west to Jacksonville and continue straight on Highway 238 for 8 miles to the settlement of Ruch. (From Grants Pass, follow signs south to Murphy and continue straight on Highway 238 to Ruch, between mileposts 25 and 26.) In Ruch, turn south toward the

Upper Applegate area for 18.8 miles. When you reach a T-shaped junction at the far end of Applegate Lake, turn left on Applegate Road for 1.2 miles to a big gravel intersection. Continue straight on one-lane Road 1050 for 0.9 mile and then fork to the right on Road 1055. Follow this narrow gravel road—not suitable for low-slung passenger cars—for 10 miles through a 2017 fire zone, climbing to Cook and Green Pass and a trailhead parking area on the right.

Two trails start on the right-hand side of this parking area. Of these, take the Pacific Crest Trail up a ridge of burned snags to the left. The snags soon give way to a rocky red scrubland of manzanita brush and beargrass. Expect views not only of Red Buttes, but also south across the Klamath River's dark canyon to the Marble Mountains and Mt. Shasta's ghostly white cone.

After 2.6 miles, at a trail junction in a brushy pass, detour 300 feet to the right to a spectacular viewpoint of green Echo Lake backed by red cliffs. If you have the time, scramble 0.5 mile down this steep, rocky side trail to Echo Lake's shore and a wildflower meadow with blue gentians.

Then return to the PCT and continue 1.5 miles to another trail junction in Lilypad Lake's scenic alpine bowl. This smaller, shallower pond is packed with yellow pond lilies. The surrounding meadow has mint, yellow sneezeweed, coneflower, and unfortunately, cow pies. As in the Swiss Alps, the background music here is often the tinny clank of cowbells.

Lilypad Lake from the Pacific Crest Trail.

From the junction near the lake, turn uphill to the right 300 feet to a viewpoint in a pass overlooking much of the Red Buttes Wilderness. At the pass you'll also find the end of an abandoned roadbed. To return on a loop, turn right on this track for a mile to a barricade near Bee Camp Spring. High clearance vehicles can drive to this point from Cook and Green Pass, but seldom do. Walking this drivable portion of the old road is no fun either, so angle left on the PCT for the final 3.1 miles back to Cook and Green Pass.

Hike 21
Grayback Mountain

On the slopes of this landmark peak you'll find a historic cabin and a glorious wildflower meadow.

Moderate (to cabin and meadow)
2.6 miles round trip
1100 feet elevation gain
Open mid-June to early November
Use: hikers, horses, bicycles

Difficult (to summit)
6.2 miles round trip
2450 feet elevation gain

The Grayback Snow Shelter.

When viewed from the Applegate Valley, Grayback Mountain looks like the broad gray back of an elephant, but it was named, however, for a much smaller animal. Miners in Southern Oregon's 1850s gold rush christened the peak after their worst bugaboo—the itchy lice commonly called graybacks.

Getting There— From Grants Pass, follow signs south 6.5 miles to Murphy and continue straight on Highway 238 another 11.5 miles to a green steel bridge at milepost 18, just before the town of Applegate. (If you're coming from Medford, follow signs for Jacksonville 5 miles west and continue straight on Highway 238 to the bridge at milepost 18.) At the bridge turn south on Thompson Creek Road for 11.9 miles. Where pavement ends at a pass, turn sharply to the right past an "O'Brien Creek Trail" sign onto Road 1005. Follow this bumpy gravel road 0.3 mile, fork left, and continue another 2 miles to a fork. The unmarked lower O'Brien Creek trailhead is uphill to the right of the creek. Stop here if you're towing a horse trailer; otherwise turn right and drive uphill another 1.7 miles to the road's end at an upper trailhead. This final rough stretch has a patch of sharp rocks that can cause flat tires, so drive slowly.

From the upper trailhead, the path climbs along an ancient roadbed for 0.2 mile before charging steeply up through dense, cool woods of old-growth

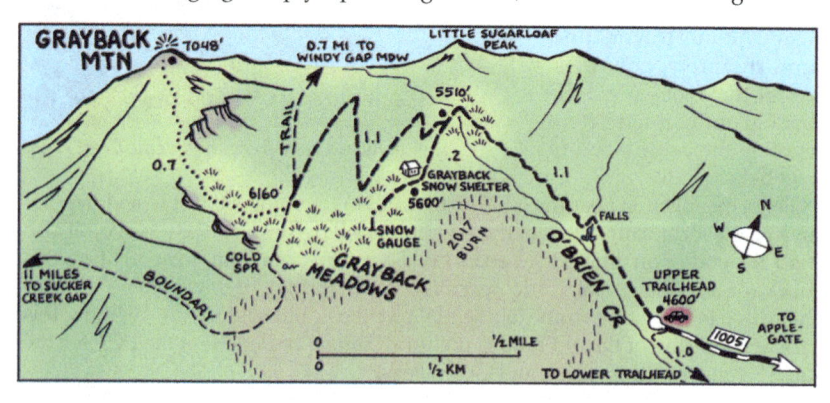

Grayback Mountain from the meadow.   Below: Rock cairn on the summit.

Douglas fir and incense cedar. At the upper end of a gully of wildflowers the path crosses O'Brien Creek.

Keep left at a fork for the level path 0.2 mile to the Grayback Snow Shelter, a 10-by-14-foot cabin with a wood floor, rustic table, folding chairs, three glassless windows, and an unlocked door. Use a knife or thin stick to lift the door's latch. The roof is tight and the loft has bunks for two. The cabin's stove should not be used in summer due to forest fire danger, so bring a backpacking stove if you want to cook. Please leave the cabin as you found it. Close the door and carry out trash. Notes at the cabin report that hikers often find a foot of snow here in mid-December. In June of 2009 a visitor named Aleksander wrote, "Only 11 years old. My dad drug me up here."

Just beyond the cabin is Grayback Meadows, abloom each summer with purple aster, goldenrod, yellow sneezeweed, orange paintbrush, and big-leaved hellebore. A campsite and snow gauge pole mark the site of a burned cabin.

If you'd like to climb Grayback Mountain, you could just bushwhack straight up this meadow, but it's probably easier to walk back to the fork in the trail and switchback uphill 1.1 mile on a path through the woods. When you reach the Boundary Trail, go left 200 feet to the meadow, and then bushwhack straight uphill to the right. Scramble through a gap in the cliffs, follow a ridgecrest, and push your way through the manzanita brush for 0.2 mile to the rocky summit.

Here a 360° panorama includes a startling, shiny swath of the Pacific Ocean near Crescent City. To the right is the woodsy Illinois Valley with the peaked ridges of the Kalmiopsis Wilderness beyond. To the left are the spires of the Siskiyou Wilderness (with M-shaped Preston Peak the tallest). Farther left are Red Buttes, snowy Mt. Shasta, Mt. McLoughlin's cone, Crater Lake's rim (above Medford), Mt. Thielsen's spire, and the Applegate Valley's ranches.

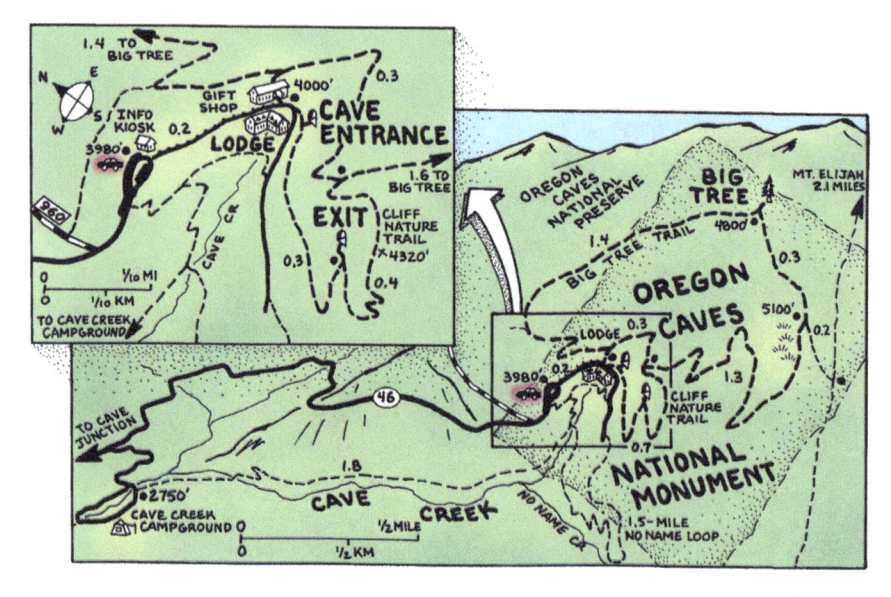

Hike 22 — Oregon Caves

Explore marble caverns underground or hike above ground to a colossal tree in this National Monument.

Easy (cave tour)
1.3-mile loop
220 feet elevation gain
Open late March to early November

Moderate (to Big Tree)
3.7-mile loop
1125 feet elevation gain
Open late April to early December

Cave entrance.

The caves won National Monument status in 1909, and the surrounding watershed was declared a National Preserve in 2015. Visitors can join a guided tour for about $10 ($7 for children 15 and under), exploring narrow passageways and stairs to hidden rooms of cave formations. For a free hike above ground try the Big Tree Loop, crossing a forested Siskiyou mountainside to one of Oregon's largest Douglas firs. Pets are banned on all park trails.

The caves' marble began as tropical island reefs in the Pacific Ocean. About 190 million years ago the advancing North American continent scraped up the island sediments to form this part of the Siskiyous. At first the land here was so wet that percolating ground water dissolved parts of the marble, forming pockets. When the land rose and the caves drained, dripping water gradually deposited calcite inside — much as a dripping faucet can stain a sink. Drips in the cave first form "soda straws," thin tubes hanging from the ceiling. When the tubes get plugged, water runs down the outsides and forms thicker stalactites.

If the drip is fast, it carries dissolved calcite to the cave floor to form a stalagmite.

Hunter Elijah Davidson discovered the cave in 1874 when his dog chased a bear into the entrance. Davidson lit matches to follow. When the last match died he found his way out of the darkness only by crawling along a cave-floor stream. After word spread of his find, early entrepreneurs damaged the cave by encouraging visitors to break off stalactites as samples and sign their names on the walls. A cave operator in the 1920s hoked up tours with ghost stories, colored lights, and hidden growling men in lion skins—the origin of the Grants Pass caveman mascot. The National Park Service now urges visitors not to touch anything in the cave. Lighting is dim to discourage the moss and algae that grow near artificial lights.

The Paradise Lost formation.

Getting There— Drive Highway 199 south from Grants Pass 29 miles (or north from Crescent City 57 miles) to Cave Junction and follow "Oregon Caves" pointers east on Highway 46 for 20 miles to a turnaround. Unless you have lodge reservations, park here and walk the road 0.2 mile to the gift shop and cave entrance.

Cave tours leave about every half hour from 9am to 6pm in summer, and about every hour from 10am to 4pm in spring and fall. There are no tours from early November to late March due to hibernating bats, and there are no tours midweek in late April or November. Tickets are available at *www.recreation.gov* or at the gift shop. Children must be 42 inches tall to join the tour. Don't bring a flashlight or a backpack, but because it averages 44° F in the cave year-round, you'll want warm clothes.

Cave entrance.

The 90-minute cave tour climbs 0.6 mile through the cave to an upper exit. From there the quickest return route is a 0.3-mile trail to the right.

If you'd rather hike to Big Tree, walk through the visitor center's breezeway arch and fork to the left. This path climbs a slope of marble outcroppings and manzanita bushes before entering old-growth fir woods with rhododendron, vanilla leaf, and incense cedar. Expect lots of golden-mantled ground squirrels, chipmunks, and dark blue Steller's jays with pointy black topknots. At Big Tree (a Douglas fir over 13 feet in diameter) the loop trail switchbacks up to the right. Keeping right at junctions you'll pass high meadows of aromatic mint, orange paintbrush, purple larkspur, and cow parsnip before descending through a grove of Port Orford cedars to the gift shop by the cave entrance.

Other Options—For a longer hike, either start 1.8 miles below the cave at Cave Creek Campground (see map), or continue up from the Big Tree Loop 2.3 miles to a viewpoint atop Mt. Elijah (see Hike #23).

Hike 23

Mount Elijah

This fun loop crosses the panoramic top of a Siskiyou peak named for Elijah Davidson, discoverer of Oregon Caves.

Moderate
5.5-mile loop
1000 feet elevation gain
Open early June to mid-November

Old sign on Mt. Elijah's summit.

A short side trip through a wildflower meadow leads to Bigelow Lake, full of lilypads. The entire watershed here was added to the Oregon Caves National Monument as a preserve in 2015, so the grazing cows are gone, and road scars have been rehabilitated. Pets are not allowed.

Getting There— Drive Highway 199 south from Grants Pass 29 miles (or north from Crescent City 57 miles) to Cave Junction and follow "Oregon Caves" pointers east on Highway 46 for 19.3 miles to road's end at the national monument's main parking lot. Turn around here, drive back just 0.1 mile, and turn steeply uphill to the right on Fire Access Road 960. After 2.9 miles on this gravel, somewhat rough road, turn right at a T-shaped junction with Road 070. In another 0.5 mile, veer uphill to the right to stay on Road 070, even though this is the smaller, rougher fork. After 0.8 mile, park at road's end *(GPS 42.1016 -123.3788)*. There is only room for five cars.

The hike begins along a rehabilitated portion of Road 070, now a level trail with young alder, maple, and fir. Wildflowers love the new route: scarlet fireweed, red paintbrush, orange tiger lily, and yellow sneezeweed. Expect butterflies too. At a mapboard after 0.6 mile, turn uphill to the left on the Lake Mountain/Bigelow Lakes Trail. If you'd like to visit the larger Bigelow Lake,

Mt. Elijah from the larger of the two Bigelow Lakes.

count the switchbacks as you hike up this path. At the fifth switchback *(GPS 42.0906 -123.3684)*, where the trail turns left beside a huge meadow, turn right across the meadow on a smaller, unofficial trail. The path peters out in a field of hellebore and sulphur plant, but continue level and straight to the head of a basin, and then veer a bit right and downhill through a boulder-strewn meadow for 0.2 mile to the shallow lake, rimmed with marshy grass, bushes of pink spirea, tall purple monkshood, and tiny white bog orchids *(GPS 42.089 -123.3706)*.

Return to the main trail and continue uphill 0.8 mile to a wooded pass. Ignore two signed side trails to the left, but at the third (unsigned!) fork, go up to the left to find the bare, rocky summit of Mt. Elijah.

View of meadows from the trail.

The 360-degree view features Mt. Shasta, a snowy ghost in the east. To its right, note the double hump of Red Buttes, the purple tooth of Preston Peak to the south, and Cave Junction's valley to the west.

Then continue straight past the summit on a rocky trail along the ridgecrest. After descending 1.3 miles, turn right at a junction with a mapboard. This path soon becomes the restored roadbed and leads 1.5 miles back to your car.

Hike 24 Eight Dollar Mountain

This conical peak looks like a volcano, but it's actually an erosional remnant with some of Oregon's oldest rocks.

Easy (boardwalk trail)
0.6 mile round trip
100 feet elevation gain
Open all year

Easy (Little Illinois River Falls)
3.3 miles round trip
300 feet elevation gain

Darlingtonia "pitcher plant".

The reddish peridotite and greenish serpentine here began as seafloor rock more than 200 million years ago. These rocks produce a soil so infertile that plants have struggled to adapt. As a result, Eight Dollar Mountain is an island of botanical diversity, home to odd bogs and rare flowers. The mountain's name dates to the 1850s gold rush, and most likely recalls a nugget unearthed along the Illinois River at the mountain's base.

All of Eight Dollar Mountain is in public or nonprofit ownership. One proposal would build an 8-mile loop trail around the peak. In the meantime you can stroll a boardwalk to a viewpoint or hike a path to a churning chute on the Illinois River.

Getting There— From Grants Pass, follow signs toward Crescent City 24 miles on Highway 199. At milepost 24 (beyond Selma 3.6 miles), turn right on Eight Dollar Road for 0.9 mile to a large parking area on the left.

Walk up a paved road to the right 0.1 mile to find the start of the 0.2-mile boardwalk. (If you have a disabled parking permit, you can drive to this upper trailhead.) The landscape here is strange in many ways. Although Eight Dollar Mountain receives more than 60 inches of rain a year, the rock has so few nutrients that the Jeffrey pine trees here are sparse and stunted.

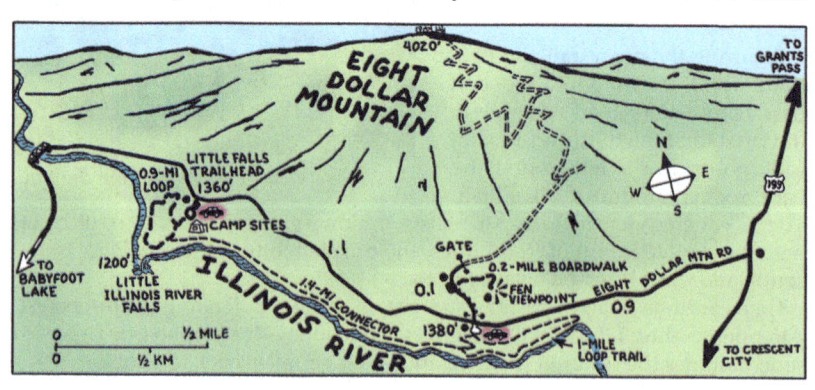

The cone-shaped mountain has virtually no creeks. Instead runoff oozes downhill through boggy slopes punctuated with the baseball-bat shapes of *Darlingtonia* pitcher plants. The viewpoint at trail's end overlooks a fen with these plants. *Darlingtonia* lures insects into its hooded throat and dissolves them to provide nitrogen and other nutrients that the soil lacks.

For the next hike from this trailhead, return to your car and take a trail downhill toward the river, keeping right at junctions. After 0.3 mile the trail crosses an old dirt road. Detour left 100 feet to the area's best beach along this green-pooled river. Then continue on the main trail, which follows the level mining flume of an ancient water ditch for most of a mile.

You'll reach an X-shaped trail junction just below a little car campground loop, where the three sites run $10 a night but have no water. Hike straight at the trail junction for a 0.9-mile loop. This route passes a *Darlingtonia* fen and then parallels the Illinois River through a rocky chasm, A rugged 100-foot side trail to the right descends to Little Illinois River Falls, a five-foot drop at the head of the gorge. A stone's throw upstream is a small beach. If you swim here, beware of the falls downstream! Then continue on the loop trail up to the X-shaped junction and turn right to return to your car.

Boardwalk through the fen.

Other Options—To learn more about the area, sign up for a class or an outing with the Siskiyou Field Institute. Allied with the Southern Oregon University Foundation, this nonprofit group runs the nearby Deer Creek nature study and research center. To find it, drive Highway 199 to the flashing yellow light in Selma (3.6 miles north of Eight Dollar Mountain Road or 20 miles south of Grants Pass), and turn west on Illinois River Road for 1.4 miles. For course offerings, tuition rates, and lodging prices at the nature center, check *www.thesfi.org* or call 541-597-8530.

Left: Little Illinois River Falls.

Hike 25 Illinois River Beaches

When summer heat sears Southern Oregon, locals flee to the swimmable green pools of the Illinois River.

Easy (Kerby Flat and Star Flat)
4.3-mile loop
560 feet elevation gain
Open all year

Easy (three other beaches)
3 miles round trip
890 feet elevation gain

Suspension footbridge.

The river's dramatic canyon has other attractions as well—weird bogs, whitewater falls, and a spectacular suspension footbridge. Only the first of the four short hikes recommended here escaped a 2018 wildfire.

Getting There— From Interstate 5 at Grants Pass, follow "Crescent City" signs south on Highway 199 for 20 miles to Selma. At a flashing yellow light, turn right on Illinois River Road for 4.3 paved miles to the well-marked Kerby Flat Trailhead, a paved pullout on the left *(GPS 42.27975 -123.6844)*.

The trail starts at the far right-hand end of a railed viewpoint and descends along a dry, rocky ridge. After 0.6 mile you'll reach a trail junction on a plateau with stunted Douglas firs and Jeffrey pines. To start the loop, turn right. This path descends past viewpoints for another 0.4 mile. Then turn sharply left on a trail that follows the Illinois River upstream, past swimmable pools.

After 0.6 mile along the river you'll reach a lovely but shadeless beach of sand

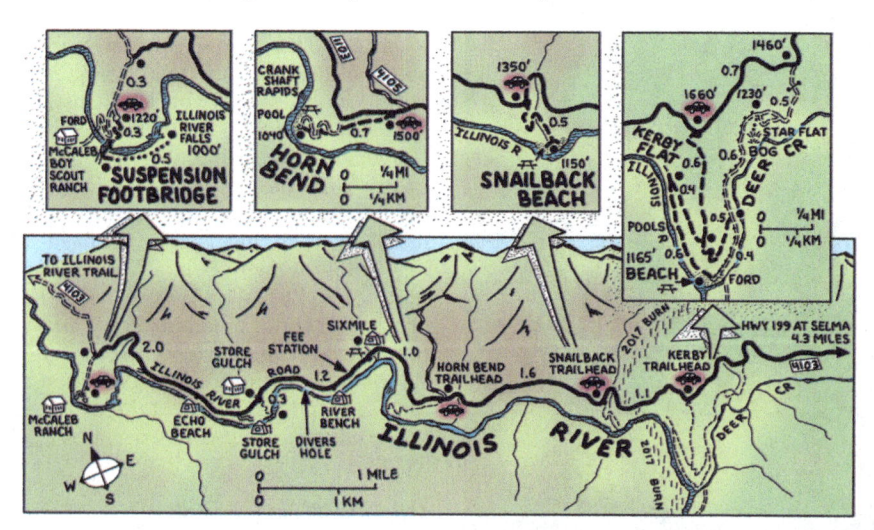

and gravel with the hike's best river access, by the mouth of Deer Creek. It's a nice spot for lunch. When you're ready to continue, follow an abandoned dirt road alongside Deer Creek. After 0.4 mile, look for a trail that climbs the hillside to the left. This is the loop route back to your car. But before heading back it's worth continuing along the road to see Star Flat's bog of insect-catching pitcher plants. To find the bog, walk another 0.6 mile along Deer Creek to a large road junction and walk back to the right through a grassy meadow 100 feet.

The next three trails to beaches have black snags from a 2018 wildfire, but some old trees survived, especially near the river. For the next hike, drive another 1.1 mile east on Illinois River Road from the Kerby Flat Trailhead to the Snailback Beach Trailhead, a pullout on the left. The half-mile path here climbs a few feet at first, but then descends a ridge and switchbacks down to Snailback Creek's confluence with the Illinois River. There are two beaches here, each with a picnic table and a swimmable pool. The beach to the left is backed by a cliff, while the beach to the right borders a river rapids with a six-foot drop.

One of the river's quietest beaches and best swimming holes is at Horn Bend. To find it from the Snailback Beach Trailhead, drive another 1.6 miles east on Illinois River Road to the Horn Bend Trailhead, a parking pullout on the left. The trail parallels the road for 0.4 mile through an area that burned in 2002 as wel l as 2018. Then you turn left down a steepish cat road, braided at times with bits of trail, for 0.3 mile to two picnic tables beside a broad sandy area. Cross the sand to find the river access, where 15-foot-deep green pools with tiny, darting fish surround rock coves, ledges, and islands.

The final recommended hike is a short path to a suspension footbridge high above the river. To find it from the Horn Bend Trailhead, drive east on Illinois River Road another 4.2 miles (and 2 miles past the crowded Store Gulch picnic/camping/swimming area). Where pavement ends, follow a pointer for the Fall Creek Trailhead straight down dirt Road 087. After 0.2 mile on this rough track, turn left into a large parking area. The trail here switchbacks down 0.3 mile to rejoin Road 087 at the dramatic, 240-foot-long, railed suspension footbridge. Although it is also possible to drive here, the road is rough and parking is tight.

The Illinois River at Kerby Flat.

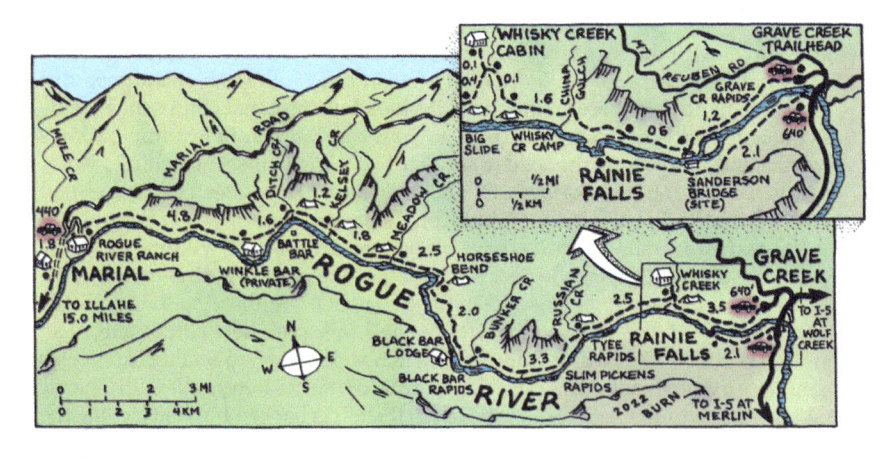

Hike 26 Rogue River Trail East

Rafting the Rogue River is an expensive permit hassle. Why not hike through this spectacular canyon instead?

Easy (to Rainie Falls)
4.2 miles round trip
180 feet elevation gain
Open all year

Moderate (to Whisky Creek)
7 miles round trip
300 feet elevation gain

Difficult (Grave Creek to Marial)
23.2 miles one way
2800 feet elevation gain

Rainie Falls.

   At times the irascible Rogue River idles along in lazy green pools, but elsewhere it's misty mayhem, plunging over Rainie Falls or boiling through Mule Creek Canyon's Coffeepot. During the peak whitewater season from May 15 to October 15, the 40-mile stretch between Grave Creek and Illahe has become such a popular float trip for kayakers and rafters that a lottery is held to issue 120 permits a day from a total of 90,000 applications (see page 16).
   Trails along the Rogue River offer the same scenery without the crowds. Day hikers can sample the canyon's eastern end with an easy walk to the 15-foot cascade at Rainie Falls. A longer day hike reaches the Whisky Creek Cabin, a gold miner's shack from 1880 restored as a rustic museum. Backpackers continuing west on the 40-mile Rogue River Trail should bring stoves because campfires are only allowed within 400 feet of the river if they're kept in firepans. At night, hang food at least 10 feet high and 5 feet from a tree trunk to discourage black bears.
   Getting There— Drive Interstate 5 north of Grants Pass 4 miles to Merlin exit 61, follow signs 3.6 miles to Merlin, and continue straight for 18.5 paved miles down the Rogue River. Beyond the settlement of Galice 7 miles (and 4.5

miles past the Rand Visitor Center), park on the right just before a high bridge across the Rogue River at Grave Creek.

The easy Rainie Falls Trail starts on the left-hand side of the road just before the bridge. Be warned that this side of the river burned in 2022, so shade is sparse. After 0.3 mile on the Rainie Falls Trail you'll pass Grave Creek Rapids, a rock-walled chute where boaters flail. At a cliffy narrows at the 1.2-mile mark, look for a sign on the far shore marking the 1964 flood's astonishing high-water level, 55 feet up. Just beyond are the cement piers of Sanderson's Bridge, a miner's mule bridge from 1907 swept away by a 1927 flood. The trail ends at a small sandy beach by Rainie Falls, where most boats are lined around the falls through a channel blasted out of the rock on the far shore for migrating fish.

For longer hikes you'll need to start on the river's north shore instead. When you're driving here from Merlin, continue across the high river bridge and turn left down to a boat ramp and parking area.

Mossy, gnarled canyon live oak trees provide a few spots of shade along this eastern portion of the Rogue River Trail. Western fence lizards do push-ups on rocks, warning other lizards away from their territory. Expect tall blue wildflowers in May: cluster lily and 6-petaled elegant brodiaea. Beware of poison oak along the trail.

Hike 1.8 miles to Rainie Falls — although this shore doesn't have as good a view as the south bank. Then continue on the main trail 1.6 miles, pass a cluster of popular campsites at a sandy beach, and cross Whisky Creek on a footbridge. Here a spur to the right leads up to the historic two-room log cabin, with its collection of rusty mining memorabilia. Note the 1890 flume ditch just uphill.

Backpackers continuing to Marial will find that the Rogue River Trail mostly traverses rocky slopes high above the river, but there are several attractions. Just 0.4 mile past Whisky Creek is Big Slide Camp, a quiet riverside tent area where a late 1800s landslide briefly dammed the Rogue, backing it up 15 miles. Highlights farther down the trail include Horseshoe Bend's dramatic river loop, Western author Zane Grey's 1926 log cabin at Winkle Bar, and the restored 1903 Rogue River Ranch museum beside the Marial trailhead.

If you'd like to stay in commercial lodges along this route, expect to pay about $175 per person per night, including meals. For the first night out, reserve well in advance at Black Bar Lodge (541-479-6507), and for the second night, aim for Marial Lodge (541-471-3262 in summer; otherwise 541-474-2057). Note that Black Bar Lodge is across the river, so you must arrange a time between 4pm and 6pm for them to pick you up by boat.

Shuttling a car from the Grave Creek trailhead to Marial requires a 35-mile drive, described in Hike #27.

The Rogue River near Grave Creek.

Hike 27 Rogue River Trail West

At Inspiration Point, the trail through the Rogue River's canyon has been blasted out of sheer basalt cliffs.

Easy (Marial to Paradise Lodge)
6.6 miles round trip
200 feet elevation gain
Open April to December

Difficult (Marial to Illahe)
15.6 miles one way
950 feet elevation gain

The Coffeepot.

Below Inspiration Point, kayaks and rafts drift through green-pooled chasms toward the roar of Blossom Bar's whitewater. In other places the Rogue River Trail ducks into forested side canyons with waterfalls. Sometimes the path emerges at grassy river bars with ancient ranch cabins and gnarled oaks. Hikers always share this wilderness gorge with the plentiful wildlife drawn by the river—kingfishers, black bears, deer, and eagles.

The eastern portion of the 40-mile Rogue River Trail is described in Hike #26. This western segment crosses the Wild Rogue Wilderness, with the river's wildest rapids and narrowest canyons. It also passes commercial lodges where hikers can stop for a meal or a night—or catch a jet boat to Gold Beach. A few warnings: Avoid August, when the rocky, exposed slopes often shimmer with 100° F heat. Poison oak is common. Backpackers should bring a stove because campfires are only allowed in no-trace firepans. At night, hang food bags at least 10 feet high and 5 feet from a tree trunk to discourage black bears.

The river's name comes from the Takelma and Tututni Indians, whom the early French trappers called *coquins* (rogues). When gold attracted white interlopers, the tribes retaliated in 1855 by massacring settlers. The Army pursued the Indians to this remote canyon, where the soldiers were besieged by a superior force of well-armed warriors. The Army's trenches are still visible above the trail at

Illahe's Big Bend Pasture. Relief troops from the east turned back when Indians rolled rocks on them from the steep slopes above Solitude Bar. When soldiers from Gold Beach arrived, however, more than a thousand Indians were taken captive and forcibly moved 150 miles north to the Siletz Reservation.

Getting There — From Interstate 5, drive 4 miles north of Grants Pass to Merlin exit 61, follow signs 3.6 miles into Merlin, and continue straight another 18.6 miles along the Rogue River through Galice. Beyond the Rand Visitor Center 4.6 miles, at the far end of a high bridge, turn briefly downhill to the left toward the Grave Creek Launch Site, but then fork uphill to the right on one-lane paved Mt. Reuben Road. After climbing 4.3 miles on Mt. Reuben Road, pavement ends. Fork to the right on gravel Road 34-8-1 for 10.3 miles to a T-shaped junction, turn right for 0.6 mile to another T-shaped junction, and and turn left on paved road 32-8-31, following signs for Marial. After another 5 miles, fork left. The final 15 miles down to Marial starts out paved, but turns to gravel and narrows to one lane.

As you approach Marial, you might detour briefly left at a sign for the Rogue River Ranch to see this farmhouse museum. Then continue on the main gravel road another

Mule Creek Canyon.

mile to a parking area on the left just before Marial Lodge. Stop here if you are driving a low-slung passenger car. Otherwise continue 0.7 mile on a rough track to the Rogue River trailhead parking lot at road's end.

The trail ahead traces the edge of Mule Creek Canyon, a gorge so narrow that boaters bridge sideways or spin in a maelstrom called The Coffeepot. After 0.7 mile the path crests at Inspiration Point, with a view across the chasm to Stair Creek's waterfalls. In another 1.4 miles the trail crosses Blossom Bar Creek, with campsites and a swimmable creek pool. Across a brushy lava flat to the left is the river's most treacherous rapids, a boulder field resembling a giant pinball game for boaters. Blossom Bar's rapids mark the upstream limit of jet boat traffic.

In another mile the trail forks at Paradise Bar's grassy airstrip. The official trail skirts the woods to the right, but keep left along the river 0.2 mile to visit Paradise Lodge, a good day-hike goal. Drop-in hikers are welcome at the bar and buffet restaurant. Book well in advance at *www.paradise-lodge.com* or 541-479-3735 if you want a room; rates are about $175 per person, including meals. Jet boats from Gold Beach (about $95 round trip) make scheduled stops at Paradise Lodge from May 15 to October 15. Call Jerry's Rogue Jets at 800-451-3645 *(www.roguejets.com)* for reservations.

If you're hiking onward from Paradise Lodge, rejoin the main trail at the upper west end of the airstrip and turn left 2.9 miles to Brushy Bar, a forested plain with a large, official campground. In the next 2.8 miles the trail skirts the cliffs of Solitude Bar and reaches Clay Hill Lodge, an inn with views and wildlife. Book rooms well in advance (*www.clayhilllodge.com,* 503-859-3772). Meals are included in the per-person price, $175 for adults and $100 for kids. From Clay Hill Lodge it's 6 miles to the Illahe trailhead, passing 20-foot Flora Dell Falls along the way.

To drive a shuttle car to Illahe from Marial, go back up the Marial road 15 miles. At an "Oregon Coast" pointer, turn left for 5 miles. At a 6-way junction, go straight on gravel Road 32-8-31 (which becomes Road 3348) for 22 miles. Then turn left on Road 33 for 15.6 miles toward Agness, and turn left toward Illahe for 3.5 miles to the trailhead spur on the right.

Crater Lake Area

*Above: Crater Lake fom Rim Village (Hike #37).
Right: The Pinnacles (Hike #41).*

*Above: Flowers at Plaikni Falls (Hike #41).
Right: Mt. Thielsen (Hike #29).
Below: Crater Lake from Sun Notch in April.*

Hike 28 — Diamond Lake

Crater Lake may be a dramatic draw for out-of-staters, but Oregonians visit neighboring Diamond Lake five times as often.

Easy (north shore)
3.4 miles round trip
No elevation gain
Open mid-May throgh November
Use: hikers, bicycles

Easy (Silent Creek)
2.3-mile loop
100 feet elevation gain

Difficult (entire lakeshore)
11.5-mile loop
100 feet elevation gain

The shore trail in April.

Diamond Lake is surrounded by mountain views, over 400 campsites, five boat ramps, a resort lodge, and a paved 11.5-mile loop trail. It's easiest to tour the John Dellenback Trail around the lake by bicycle, but a quiet section along the lake's north shore makes a lovely stroll, and the beautiful, unpaved spur trail through the wildflower meadows of glassy Silent Creek is open only to foot traffic.

The 3,015-acre lake has an average depth of only 20 feet, so it becomes swimmably warm in August. It's also stocked with rainbow trout. Jet skis are banned and boats have a 10 mph limit. Mosquitoes are a problem in June and early July.

Diamond Lake's basin once cradled a broad Ice Age glacier that descended

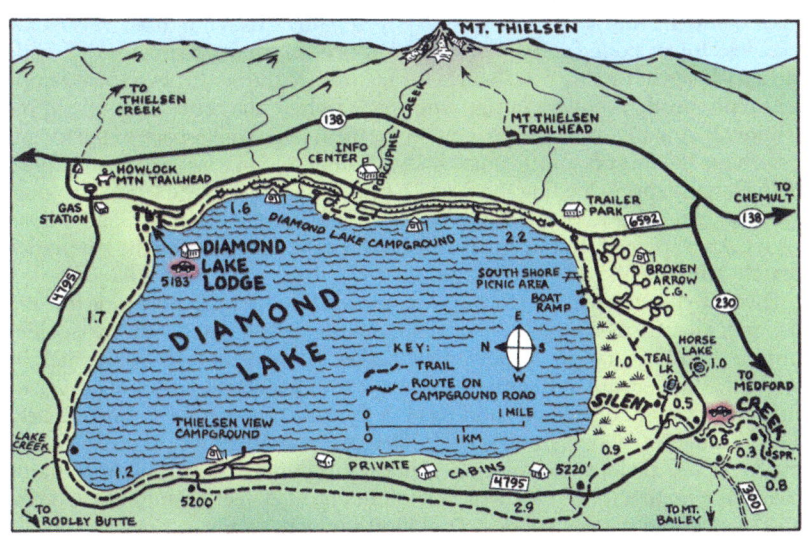

85

from the flanks of Mt. Thielsen, Mt. Bailey, and Crater Lake's volcano, Mt. Mazama. A lake had replaced the glacier by the time Mt. Mazama's eruption sent a glowing avalanche of frothy pumice and hot gases racing toward the North Umpqua River canyon. The lake did not vaporize under that hot blast, perhaps because earlier eruptions had left a blanket of pumice floating on the lake as an insulating bridge.

Getting There— Diamond Lake Lodge makes a good starting point for a lakeshore tour. To find it, turn off either Highway 138 or Highway 230 at "Diamond Lake Recreation Area" signs and follow paved Road 6592 to a "Lodge" pointer. Turn here and drive past the boat ramp before parking on the left at the lodge. The compound includes not only a restaurant and store, but also a marina shop where you can rent boats and bicycles.

If you're hiking, simply walk to the sandy picnic beach in front of the lodge, follow the lakeshore to the right, and climb to the paved bike path. If you're pedaling, bike from the lodge parking lot directly away from the lake (past a "Dead End" sign) for 0.1 mile to the paved path on the left.

Ducks, trout, and zillions of dragonflies patrol the lapping shore. Raucous gray jays and golden-mantled ground squirrels watch passersby. Look on the grassy banks for tiny blue forget-me-nots and large mountain bluebells (*mertensia*). At times the trail dips into a forest of Douglas fir, lodgepole pine, and long needled ponderosa pine. Look here for white trilliums in May and star-flowered solomonseal in June. Views ahead are to broad Mt. Bailey. Spire-tipped Mt. Thielsen (Hike #29) is behind you. After 1.7 miles, the trail briefly joins a road to cross Lake Creek, the lake's outlet. This is a good turnaround spot for hikers with children. If you're continuing, you'll find the trail wedged between the shore and the road for the next 1.2 miles. Beyond this the paved path crosses the road, traverses a viewless forest slope for 2.9 miles to avoid private cabins, recrosses the road, strikes off across brushy marshlands for 1.9 miles to the South Shore boat ramp, and then mostly follows campground roads (where the route is identified by painted bike symbols on the pavement) for the final 3.8 miles back to the lodge.

Perhaps the most beautiful short hike at Diamond Lake follows Silent Creek to the largest spring feeding the lake. To find this unpaved trail from Diamond Lake Lodge, drive 2.7 miles south on Road 6592, turn right at a "South Shore Picnic Area" pointer, follow Road 4795 for 1.5 miles, and park on the left immediately after the Silent Creek bridge.

This path heads upstream through an oasis in the dry lodgepole pine forests. In June, Silent Creek's mossy banks are ablaze with white marsh marigolds, purple shooting stars, and yellow violets. Alas, the mosquitoes here are thickest when the flowers are at their best. After the trail passes the spring it curves to the right through dry woods and meets a faint dirt road at the 1.4-mile mark. The official trail follows this track left 300 feet to a dusty trailhead on Road 300, but for a pleasant loop route back to your car, turn right instead. Follow the faint road 0.3 mile to its end, bushwhack straight ahead 20 feet through the woods, and turn left on the Silent Creek Trail for 0.6 mile to your car.

Mt. Thielsen from the lake.

Hike 29   Mount Thielsen

Towering above Diamond Lake, Mt. Thielsen's spire commands views from Mt. Shasta to the Three Sisters.

Difficult (to Pacific Crest Trail)
7.6 miles round trip
1950 feet elevation gain
Open end of July through October

Very Difficult (to summit)
10 miles round trip
3800 feet elevation gain

Mt. Thhielsen's summit view.

A popular path climbs to the Pacific Crest Trail on Mt. Thielsen's flank. Hardy hikers can continue to a dizzying ledge at the base of the summit spire, and many dare to scale the final pitch as well.

Originally a broad, 11,000-foot volcano, Mt. Thielsen stopped erupting about 100,000 years ago when a lava plug blocked its throat. Since then, erosion by Ice Age glaciers has left this hard lava core exposed as the summit spire. The peak's nickname, "Lightning Rod of the Cascades," reflects both its shape and its weather. Lightning has left the summit boulders spattered with black *fulgurite*—glassy recrystalized rock. The name Thielsen (pronounced *TEEL-sun*) honors a Danish-American pioneer railroad engineer.

Getting There—From Medford, take Highway 62 east and follow "Diamond Lake" signs a total of 81 miles. At that point *do not* take the "Diamond Lake Recreation Area" turnoff. Instead continue 0.1 mile to a "Roseburg" pointer and turn left onto Highway 138. In 1.4 miles you'll find the Mt. Thielsen Trailhead parking area on the right. If you're coming from Roseburg, take Highway 138 east for 81.6 miles. Ignore a "Diamond Lake Recreation Area" turnoff and continue 3 miles to the large trailhead sign on the left.

A parking permit is required. If you don't have a Northwest Forest Pass you

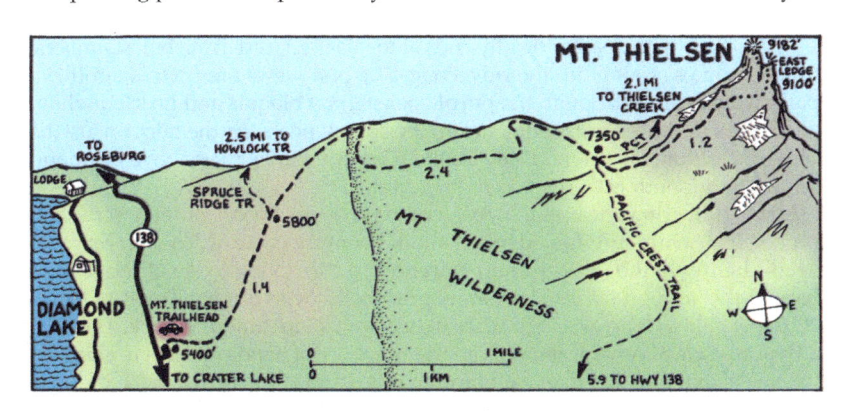

Mt. Thielsen from the trail.

can pay the $5-per-car-per-day fee at a box at the trailhead.

The trail climbs a dry, sparsely forested ridge, so bring plenty of water. As you gain elevation, lodgepole pine trees and manzanita bushes give way to mountain hemlock and red huckleberry. Notice how the trail cut exposes tan pumice gravel blasted here by the eruption of Crater Lake's Mt. Mazama 7700 years ago. Since then, only an inch or two of forest duff has managed to form atop the debris.

After 3.8 miles the path officially ends at the Pacific Crest Trail, but a climbers' trail continues straight up the ridgecrest. The best views are up this unofficial path, which climbs through the purple penstemon blooms and gnarled whitebark pines of timberline. To the north, the snowy peaks on the horizon are the Three Sisters and Diamond Peak. To the west, Mt. Bailey rises above Diamond Lake. To the south is Crater Lake's jagged rim.

Above timberline the braided, rocky path gives out amidst slippery scree and broken rock. Only sure-footed hikers should venture upward. The correct route veers slightly to the right, spiraling around to a dizzying ledge at the eastern base of the summit spire. This ledge, practically overhanging Thielsen Creek 2000 feet below, is an excellent place to declare victory and turn back. The final 80 feet are nearly vertical and require the adept use of hands and feet to chimney up cracks in the rock. Hikers attempting this do so at their own risk.

Hike 30 National Creek Falls

The very easy trail to this cool, misty waterfall glen is a nice stop on your way to Crater Lake.

Easy
0.8 mile round trip
170 feet elevation gain
Open mid-April through November

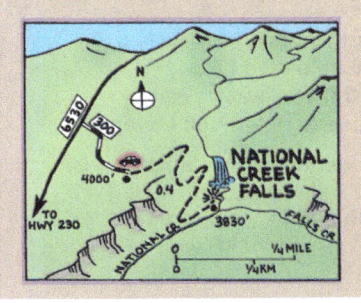

National Creek has been a favorite stop for travelers since the 1860s, when miners and stockmen blazed a route past here on their way from Southern Oregon to the newly discovered John Day gold fields.

Getting There — From Medford, drive Crater Lake Highway 62 east 57 miles; just beyond Union Creek, fork left onto Highway 230 toward Diamond Lake. After 6 more miles, at a sign marking the Jackson County line, turn east on paved Road 6530 for 1.3 miles. Then fork left to keep on Road 6530 for another 2.4 miles, and finally turn right on a dirt road for 0.2 mile to the trailhead at road's end.

The trail sets off through woods of mixed Douglas fir, hemlock, flat-needled grand fir, and white pine. Look on the trail for spiny golf-ball-sized "porcupine eggs" —the seed of the broadleaf chinkapin trees that form a scraggly understory here. In May, Oregon grape has clusters of yellow flowers and vanilla leaf puts up fuzzy white flower stalks resembling bottle brushes.

National Creek Falls.

After ambling 0.2 mile the trail passes the top of the falls. Don't venture near the cliffs for a view. Instead continue down the trail another 0.2 mile to its end at the base of the falls, a side-by-side pair of 80-foot fans that spray out over a basalt cliff. The rock is actually the broken edge of a lava flow from Mt. Mazama, Crater Lake's ancient volcano.

Hike 31 — Union Creek

From the rustic resort village of Union Creek, hike along the stream to a series of small, mossy waterfalls.

Easy (to falls from Road 610)
0.6 mile round trip
120 feet elevation gain
Open April through November

Moderate (to falls from Hwy 62)
8.2 miles round trip
330 feet elevation gain

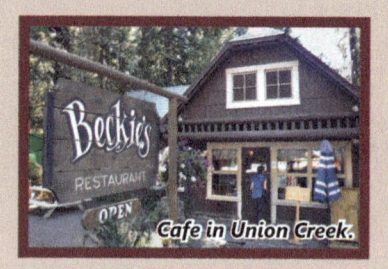

Cafe in Union Creek.

The middle part of the 4.1-mile path from the Union Creek Campground to the falls can be brushy and unmaintained. If you're pressed for time, a backdoor route will take you to the falls in just 0.3 mile.

Getting There — Begin by driving Crater Lake Highway 62 east from Medford. At milepost 56, turn left into the Union Creek Campground entrance and immediately park in a large lot on the right. This is the start of the longer hiking route up Union Creek.

At the left end of the parking lot, cross Union Creek on a footbridge to a historic picnic shelter built by the Civilian Conservation Corps in the 1930s. Then walk to the right (upstream) through the trees 300 feet to Beckie's Restaurant. Carefully cross Highway 62 and walk around the left side of the Union Creek lodge and store. Behind the lodge 200 feet, beside Cabin #21, you'll find the path heading upstream along Union Creek.

Union Creek Falls is a series of small cascades.

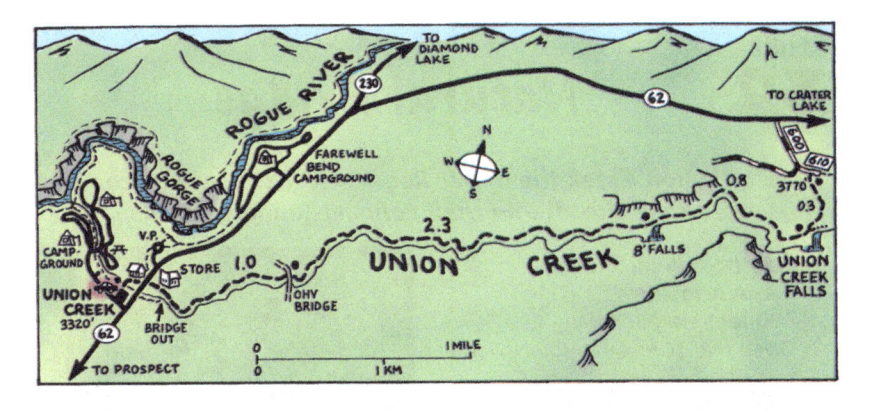

The Douglas firs in these woods are as much as 7 feet in diameter. The scraggly, flat-needled trees along the creek are yew; its bark yields the cancer drug taxol, and its resilient wood was once used by Indians for bows. Bracken fern and vanilla leaf add greenery to the forest floor.

After a mile, beyond a bridge for off-highway vehicles, the trail can be poorly maintained. If the path is clear, you'll notice that the creek now bubbles through miniature waterfalls and gorges. Watch for ouzels near an 8-foot cascade at the 3.3-mile mark. These dark gray, robin-sized birds dive underwater in search of insect larvae.

Shelter at the campground.

In another 0.8 mile you'll reach the start of Union Creek Falls, and a fork that leads to the upper trailhead.

If you'd rather start your hike at this easier upper trailhead, drive Highway 62 north of Union Creek 1.3 miles, veer right on Highway 62 toward Crater Lake for 2 miles, turn right on gravel Road 600 for 0.2 mile, and fork left on dirt Road 610 for 0.1 mile to the trailhead at road's end.

After 0.3 mile the trail forks at the creek. Union Creek Falls is not a single waterfall, but rather a series of water slides, chutes, and rock channels. You'll find some of this water magic downstream, on the trail to the resort, and some upstream, on a trail that soon peters out at a small cascade.

91

Hike 32

Natural Bridge

Near Union Creek the upper Rogue River squeezes through a rock chasm and then vanishes underground.

Easy (to Natural Bridge)
2.4-mile loop
300 feet elevation gain
Open mid-March through November

Easy (Rogue Gorge to Union Creek)
2.2-mile loop
No elevation gain

Union Creek foorbridge.

Easy loop hikes visit each of these daredevil performances by the irascible Rogue. If you'd like to see both of the river's stunts, a moderate 8-mile hike combines the two loops in one.

The secret behind both of the river's magic tricks is its use of lava tubes. Several thousand years ago Crater Lake's volcano filled this canyon with a long basalt lava flow. When the lava's crusted surface stopped moving, the molten rock underneath kept on flowing, leaving long caves. At Natural Bridge the Rogue River funnels through one of these tubes like water through a hose. At Rogue Gorge the river has ripped open the cave's roof, leaving a slot of raging whitewater.

Getting There — Drive Crater Lake Highway 62 east from Medford 55 miles (or west of Union Creek 1.1 mile), and turn off the highway at a "Natural Bridge Campground" sign near milepost 55. Then keep left for 0.7 mile to the Natural Bridge day use parking area. The trail starts at an information kiosk at the far right-hand end of the lot.

The paved path crosses the river on a long footbridge. Pavement ends in 0.2 mile at a railed viewpoint of the natural bridge. Below, the frothing river appears to be sucked into solid rock. Water pressure in the 200-foot lava tube is so great that spray sputters out from cracks in the cave roof.

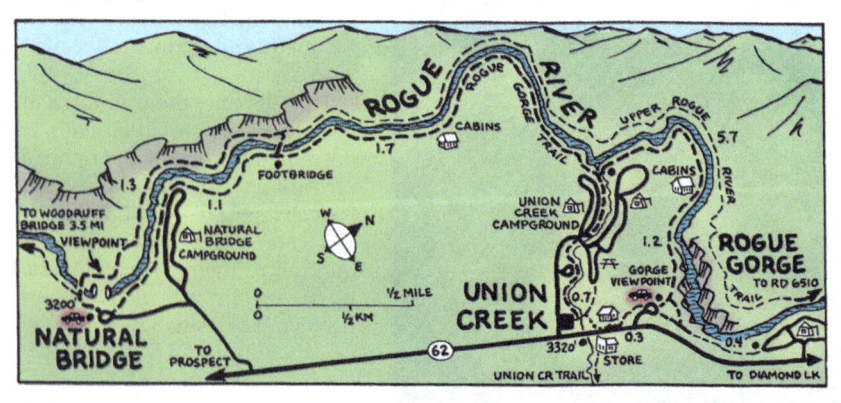

Rogue River footbridge on the Natural Bridge loop.

Most tourists turn back here. But a lovely, quiet portion of the Upper Rogue River Trail continues upstream. In early summer, large patches of 5-petaled white anemones bloom here beneath old Douglas firs. Also look for vanilla leaf, with three big leaves and a stalk of tiny white flowers.

A mile beyond Natural Bridge take a fork to the right, cross the river on a footbridge over a churning chasm, and come to a T-junction with the Rogue Gorge Trail. Only turn left if you're interested in the 8-mile hike combining both loops. To complete the first short loop, turn right and hike 1.1 mile to your car.

The other easy loop hike, to Rogue Gorge, is a more civilized tour, passing summer cabins, campgrounds, and a cafe in the resort village of Union Creek. To start, drive Highway 62 to Union Creek at milepost 56. A few hundred feet north of town, follow a "Rogue Gorge" sign to a parking lot. First take a minute to explore a paved 0.2-mile loop trail that visits fenced viewpoints of the 100-foot-deep gorge. This is all most tourists will see. For a more thorough, 2.2-mile tour of the Union Creek area, however, follow the fence downstream and continue on the unpaved Rogue Gorge Trail.

After 1.2 miles along the wooded riverbank, cross a footbridge over Union Creek to a trail junction. To the right the Rogue Gorge Trail continues 1.7 miles along the river to the Natural Bridge loop described above. For the short loop back to your car, however, turn left along Union Creek. This creekside path actually goes through a few campground sites, but the campers know they're beside a trail and don't seem to mind passersby. After stubbornly following the creekbank 0.7 mile upstream, turn left along Highway 62. Just beyond Beckie's Restaurant, angle left beside a propane tank on a short trail back to your car.

Hike 33
Takelma Gorge

Tormented by an ancient lava flow, the Rogue River foams for a mile through this 150-foot-deep rock slot.

Easy (to Takelma Gorge)
3.2 miles round trip
100 feet elevation gain
Open March to mid-December

Easy (to River Bridge, with shuttle)
4.6 miles one way
160 feet elevation gain

Oregon grape is the state flower.

Several thousand years ago, Crater Lake's volcano filled the Rogue's valley with 650 feet of lava and ash. Through Takelma Gorge the river follows a crack in the lava—a weak spot where water eroded a canyon.

The gorge is named for the Upland Takelma (or Latgawa), a tribe native to this area. They often raided the Lowland Takelma in what is now the Grants Pass area for food and slaves. In their Penutian language—unrelated to the languages of other Southern Oregon tribes—Takelma means "those who live by the river." Early French trappers called them *coquins* ("rogues"), and later white settlers dubbed them Rogue River Indians. Today the Upper Rogue River Trail wends through an old-growth forest along the gorge's rim.

Getting There— Drive north and then east from Medford on Crater Lake Highway 62. Between mileposts 51 and 52 (past the Prospect Ranger Station 6 miles) turn left onto paved Woodruff Meadows Road 68. After 1.7 miles turn left into the Woodruff Bridge picnic area, a parking pullout just before the bridge.

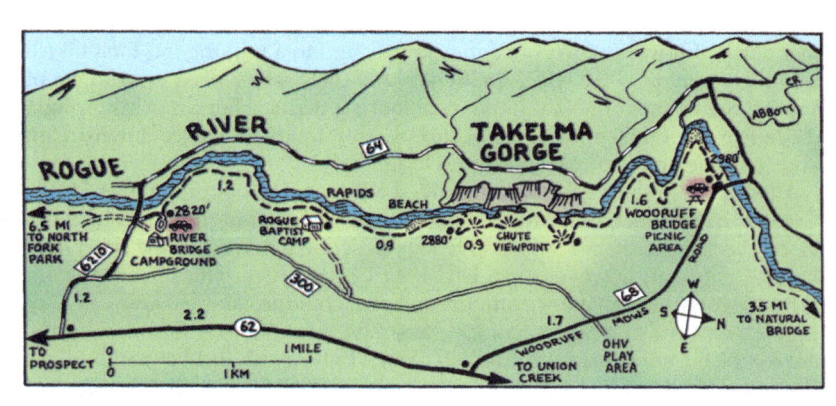

Start by walking down to the right 100 feet to see a 6-foot waterfall beneath the river bridge. A sandy beach just downstream is popular with kids. Then climb back to the picnic area and head downriver on a trail among 7-foot-thick Douglas fir. In early summer look here for tiny white starflower, the delicate double bells of twinflower, 5-petaled white anemone, and yellow Oregon grape blooms. In fall, vine maple lines the river with scarlet pinwheel-shaped leaves.

After 1.6 miles the trail reaches the first Takelma Gorge viewpoint, on a clifftop above the spectacular, churning chasm, where the river twists around a hairpin curve and rages down a chute. Hikers with small children could turn back here, but it would take willpower, because the next 0.9 mile of trail follows the gorge's rim past a succession of stunning viewpoints. Finally the trail switchbacks down to a tamer stretch of river. In another 0.3 mile the path passes a small sandy beach suitable for sunning or wading—another possible turnaround point.

If you'd like to hike the entire 4.6-mile trail section from Woodruff Bridge to River Bridge one way, plan to leave a shuttle car at the far end. To find that trailhead, turn off Highway 62 a ways south of milepost 51. Take gravel Road 6210 west 1 mile, turn right into the River Bridge Campground entrance, and keep left for 0.2 mile to a trail sign at the day-use parking area.

Takelma Gorge.

Other Options—
Long-range hikers can continue along the Upper Rogue River Trail for days. If you're walking downstream, it's 6.5 miles to trail's end at North Fork Park. (To find this trailhead, drive 0.4 mile south of the Prospect Ranger Station on Highway 62 and turn right on a gravel road beside a canal for half a mile.) The trail is prettier upstream, however. From Woodruff Bridge it's 3.5 miles to Natural Bridge (Hike #32) and 36.8 miles to the Mount Mazama Viewpoint trailhead near the Rogue River's source at Boundary Springs.

Hike 34 — Annie Creek

Wildflowers, brooks, and ash pinnacles highlight two short loop trails near Crater Lake's Mazama Campground.

Easy (Annie Creek Canyon)
1.7-mile loop
200 feet elevation gain
Open mid-June through November

Easy (Godfrey Glen)
1-mile loop
50 feet elevation gain

Golden-mantled ground squirrel.

The trailheads for the two paths are just 2 miles apart, so it's easy to hike them both in a day. Pets are allowed at Godfrey Glen, but not at Annie Creek.

Getting There— The 1.7-mile loop through Annie Creek Canyon starts in the national park's largest campground. If you're staying here, simply walk to the end of the "D" or "E" loop and follow signs to the amphitheater. If you're driving here, head north from the Highway 62 park entrance for 0.3 mile, turn right onto the Mazama Campground entrance road, keep right, and park in front of the store. A trailhead is planned here. If you don't see it, walk through the campground to the amphithreater at the end of loop D.

Behind the amphitheater, turn right on a trail that follows the wooded rim of Annie Creek's canyon along the edge of the campground. Black bears do visit these woods daily, looking for campsites with obvious cooler chests, but you're unlikely to see these unaggressive bears. On the other hand, you're almost certain to spot three species of squirrels and chipmunks. The lively, orange-bellied Douglas squirrels have no stripes and often chatter in trees. Golden-mantled ground squirrels have striped sides and scamper into burrows. Genuine chipmunks are smaller and have side stripes that extend all the way past their eyes.

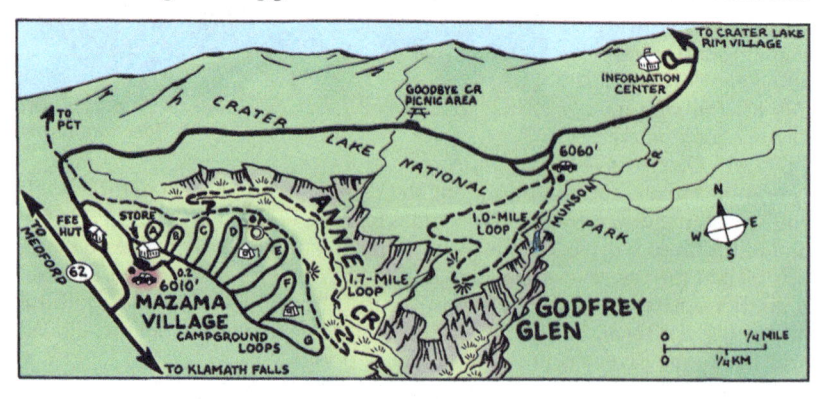

After skirting the campground for 0.4 mile the Annie Creek Trail switchbacks down into a canyon with several weird-looking ash pinnacles. The story behind the pinnacles begins in the Ice Age, when glaciers scoured U-shaped valleys through Annie Creek's canyon and adjacent Godfrey Glen. After the ice retreated, the eruption of Crater Lake's Mt. Mazama filled both valleys to the brim with glowing avalanches of hot pumice and ash. When the debris stopped, superheated gas rose through it, welding ash into solid rock along the vents. Since then streams have cut narrow V-shaped canyons into the softer ash, exposing the old vents as spires.

Beyond the ash pinnacles the path follows the lovely cascading stream up through wildflower meadows a mile before climbing back to the loop's start at the amphitheater.

To take the all-accessible 1-mile loop hike to Godfrey Glen, drive back to the park's main entrance road, turn right toward Rim Village for 2.1 miles, and turn right at a "Godfrey Glen Nature Loop" sign for 0.1 mile to the trailhead. The trail here promptly forks for the loop; keep left for the quickest route to the astonishing overlook of Godfrey Glen, a green oasis 300 feet below in a box canyon flanked by fluted spires of beige ash. Watch children near this dangerously unrailed viewpoint. Then continue on the loop through the woods to your car.

Annie Creek.

Godfrey Glen.

Hike 35   Park Headquarters

When you stop at Crater Lake's visitor center, stretch your legs with two short walks—one to a wildflower meadow and one to historic park buildings.

Easy (Lady of the Woods Loop)
0.5-mile loop
120 feet elevation gain
Open mid-June through November

Easy (Castle Crest wildflowers)
1.2-mile loop
70 feet elevation gain

The visitor center.

The park's Steel Visitor Information Center has lots of interesting displays inside, but the best displays are outside. The half-mile Lady of the Woods loop visits a dozen historic stone buildings in the adjacent forest. Just across the street, a 1.2-mile hike takes you to the park's best wildflower meadow, amid the mossy springs of Castle Crest. Pets are allowed on the Lady of the Woods Loop, but not at Castle Crest.

Getting There— Drive north from Highway 62 for 3.8 miles (or south from Rim Village 2.6 miles). At a stop sign, turn into the park headquarters parking lot. The Steel Visitor Information Center here, built of massive stones and timbers in the rustic national park style, opened in 1932 as a ranger dormitory. Now it's a visitor center with displays, books, brochures, and helpful rangers. Booklets describing the two loop hikes are available at the trailheads for 25 cents.

To find the first trailhead, walk around the left-hand end of the visitor information building. Then cross a footbridge over a branch of Munson Creek and fork uphill to the right on a dirt path into the woods. After 0.1 mile you'll reach a post marked #3. A doctor visiting the park in 1917 spent two weeks chiseling a reclining nude into a boulder here. Early park guides touted the unfinished sculpture as a tourist attraction under the name "The Lady of the Woods."

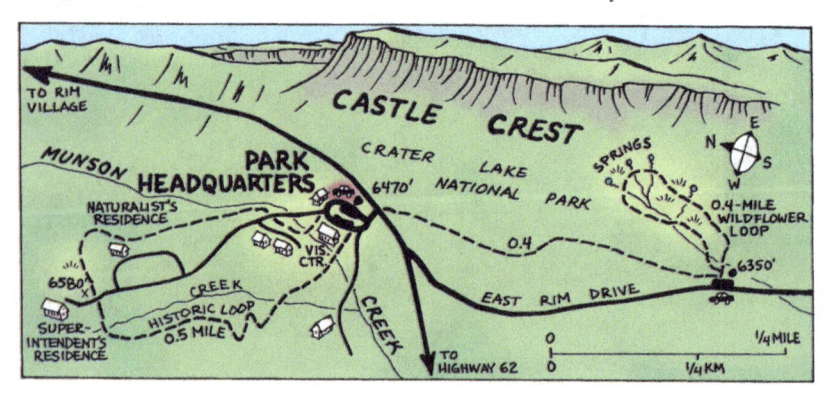

Stone steps on the Castle Crest loop.   Below: Monkeyflowers by the springs.

Next the loop switchbacks up alongside a woodsy creek and crosses the driveway of the 1933 superintendent's residence, now renovated as a educational center. At this point the path enters a creekside meadow with pink monkeyflower, purple aster, green hellebore, yellow groundsel, and views of Castle Crest's cliff. The historic tour route passes below the 1932 naturalist's residence and crosses a road beside a row of mid-1920s employee residences before returning to the visitor center parking lot.

The second short hike at park headquarters tours the wildflower meadow at Castle Crest. If you're short on time you can drive to the start of the loop by turning right 0.1 mile on the highway and forking left on Rim Drive 0.4 mile to a pullout on the left, just beyond a "Congested Area" sign.

But why not leave your car where it is and take a connector trail instead? From the entrance to the visitor center parking lot, simply walk across the highway on a crosswalk and follow a path through the trees 0.4 mile to the Castle Crest parking pullout, where the loop itself begins.

Walk the loop counter-clockwise. Start by crossing a 10-foot-wide branch of Munson Creek and climbing to a mossy slope of springs and flowers.

The pink blooms here are trumpet-shaped monkeyflowers and dart-shaped shooting stars. The blue flowers are pea-like lupines, tiny forget-me-nots, and elephant heads—stalks clustered with scores of tiny blooms that really look like elephant heads. The white ball-shaped flowers are American bistort.

The loop crosses the creek twice more before returning to the parking pullout—and the 0.4-mile connector back to the visitor center.

Hike 36

Garfield Peak

Perhaps the prettiest trail in Crater Lake National Park follows the lake's craggy rim from the historic lodge to the wildflowers and views of Garfield Peak.

Moderate
3.4 miles round trip
1010 feet elevation gain
Open mid-July through October

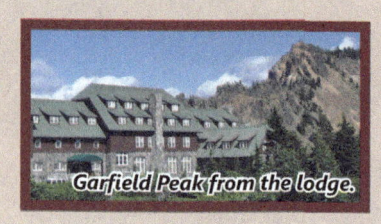

Garfield Peak from the lodge.

This is a mountain climb easy enough for kids—and it starts at the lodge patio where you can order ice cream or drinks. Pets and flower-picking are banned.

Getting There— The path begins at the back porch of the grand old Crater Lake Lodge. To find it, follow signs to Crater Lake's Rim Village and continue straight through this beehive of tourists 0.3 mile to a turnaround at road's end.

Truth be told, the lodge here wasn't always grand. Built from 1909-1915 at a cost of just $50,000, the building originally opened with tarpaper on its outside walls and flimsy beaverboard between rooms. Years of makeshift maintenance and harsh winters left the building slated for demolition in the 1980s. But a public outcry pushed the Park Service to renovate it instead. After a $35 million makeover, the lodge reopened in 1995 with elegant woodwork in the Great Hall, a modern bath in each guestroom, and its rustic ambiance remarkably intact.

Walk behind the lodge and turn right on the paved pathway along Crater Lake's rim. Pavement soon yields to a broad trail through meadows of pale blue lupine, bright orange paintbrush, yellow groundsel, purple daisy-shaped fleabane, and white pearly everlasting. Views improve with each switchback. The trail climbs past cliffs of *breccia*—welded volcanic rubble from Mt. Mazama's early mountain-building eruptions. The breccia here was long buried with lava flows, but these were stripped away by glaciers. The glaciers, in turn, vanished

Crater Lake Lodge's patio.   Below: The trail up Garfield Peak.

after Mt. Mazama lost its summit in a cataclysmic blast 7700 years ago.

Snow patches linger across the trail until August near the top. At this elevation, only gnarled, 5-needle whitebark pines survive. These trees' limber limbs, so flexible they can be tied in knots, help the pines bend rather than break in winter gales.

Garfield Peak was named for the Interior Secretary of Teddy Roosevelt, who created the national park in 1902. When you reach the peak's summit, the glowing blue of Crater Lake gapes below like a 4-cubic-mile pool from a high-dive tower. If you're quiet you might see foot-long marmots and guinea-pig-sized pikas watching from cliff-edge rocks 100 feet north of the summit. To the east, Mt. Scott looms above Phantom Ship's small craggy island. To the south stretch the distant flats of Klamath Lake, with the tip of Mt. Shasta and the cone of Mt. McLoughlin to the right.

Hike 37
Discovery Point

Explore the shattered flank of Crater Lake's ancient Mt. Mazama with either of two very different hikes from Rim Village.

Easy (to Discovery Point)
2.2 miles round trip
100 feet elevation gain
Open July through October

Difficult (fto Lightning Spring)
12.9-mile loop
1900 feet elevation gain

Clark's nutcracker.

Start with an easy view-packed stroll from Rim Village to Discovery Point. If you're gung-ho, continue on a much longer loop that descends past Lightning Spring and returns through forests. Those who plan to backpack on this longer loop will need to pick up an overnight permit at a national park office. Pets are not allowed.

Getting There — Start in Rim Village at the big paved parking area by the gift shop. Take the sidewalk to the left along Crater Lake's rim, heading clockwise around the lake. The pavement and the tourist crowds soon end. After 0.1 mile you'll briefly follow the Rim Road's shoulder. Then the path swerves back to the caldera rim for 0.7 mile of glorious views.

The picture-postcard setting features cone-shaped Wizard Island below the massive dacite cliffs of Llao Rock, with a frame of gnarled whitebark pines and mountain hemlocks. Look for lavender cushions of 5-petaled phlox along the path and raucous gray-and-black Clark's nutcrackers in the trees.

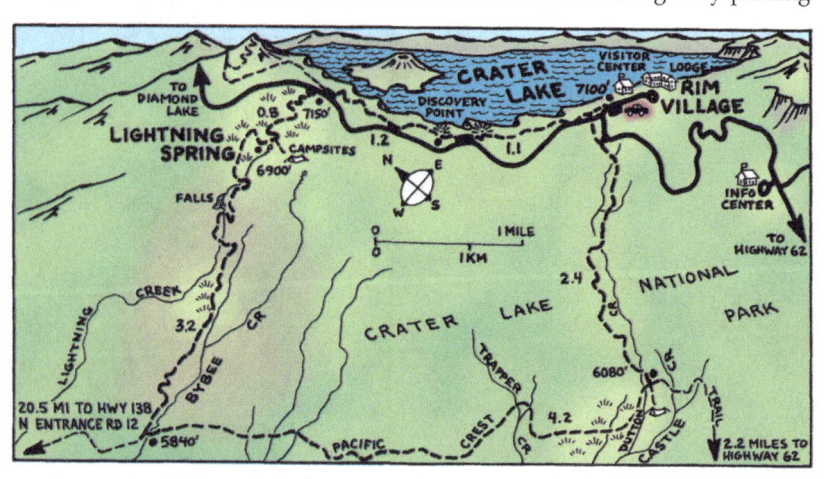

At the 1-mile mark the trail switchbacks down to cross a highway parking pullout. Then it climbs 0.1 mile to Discovery Point, where a bronze plaque commemorates the viewpoint from which John Wesley Hillman's prospecting party may have first spotted the lake in 1853.

For the easy hike, turn back here. If you're ready to tackle the longer loop, however, continue 1.2 miles along the rim-edge trail. When you reach the third highway parking pullout, cross the road and walk 300 feet along it to the gravel Lightning Springs trailhead on the left. This path — actually a long-abandoned roadbed — descends a dry, sandy slope in sweeping curves. Mt. Mazama's pumice and ash fell so deep here 7700 years ago that only a few lupine, phlox, and dogbane plants have yet taken hold. After 0.8 miles you'll pass Lightning Spring, where a deliciously cold, 3-foot-wide creek emerges from the dry slope.

Beyond the spring the trail descends a valley amid woods that burned in 2016. After 0.8 mile you'll pass a 15-foot waterfall. In another 2.4 miles you'll meet the Pacific Crest Trail — one of the few trails in the national park where horses (and dogs on leash) are allowed. Turn left on this level but relatively dull route through lodgepole pine woods for 4.2 miles. At an X-shaped junction by scenic Dutton Creek, turn left for the 2.4-mile climb back to Rim Village. This last section starts amid lovely meadowed openings of blue lupine, scarlet gilia, green hellebore, and chattering songbirds. Then it crosses 6-foot-wide Castle Creek and climbs more seriously through mountain hemlock woods back to Rim Village.

Crater Lake from Discovery Point.   Above: Lightning Spring.

Hike 38 — The Watchman

High on Crater Lake's western rim, The Watchman's lookout tower commands an eagle's-eye view across the amazingly blue lake to Wizard Island.

Easy (to Watchman Lookout)
1.6 miles round trip
420 feet elevation gain
Open mid-July through October

Easy (past Hillman Peak)
4 miles round trip
250 feet elevation gain

The Watchman's patio.

   The steep little climb up The Watchman is one of the most popular paths in the national park. It's also short enough that you might want to extend the hike by taking an adjacent 2-mile path around Hillman Peak to a viewpoint above the Devils Backbone. Pets are not allowed.
   The Watchman won its name in 1886, when the U.S. Geological Survey set up a watch point here while surveyors in a boat sounded the lake with a reel of piano wire. Other names that stuck from that 1886 expedition are Cleetwood Cove (for the boat) and Dutton Cliff (for its captain). The survey recorded a maximum lake depth of 1996 feet—a figure that has since been corrected by sonar to 1943 feet.
   Getting There— The Watchman Trail begins at a large, rail-fenced parking area and viewpoint on Crater Lake's West Rim Drive. The parking area is not well marked, but you'll find it by driving 4 miles north of Rim Village or 2.2 miles south of the junction with the north entrance road. From the parking area, follow a paved sidewalk along the highway 300 feet south to the actual trailhead. Look here for the fuzzy seedheads of western pasque flower and the blue trumpets of penstemon.
   The wide path—a portion of the long-abandoned 1917 rim road—traverses

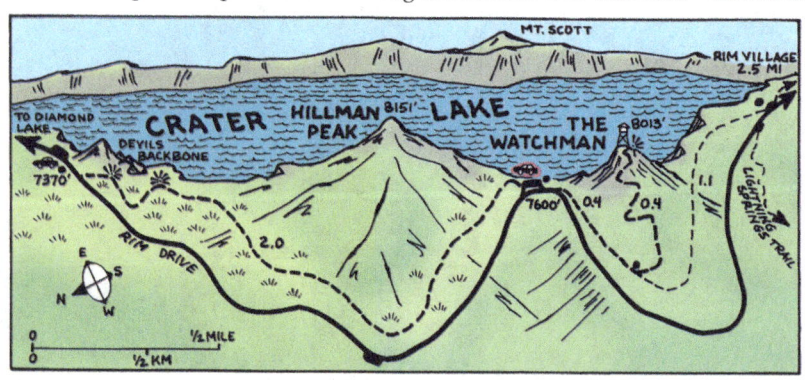

Wizard Island from The Watchman.   Below: The same view in April.

a rockslide of giant cream-colored boulders. These rocks are dacite, originally part of a 50,000-year-old lava flow on Mt. Mazama's shoulder. After Mazama's cataclysmic decapitation 7700 years ago, the old lava flow was left as The Watchman, a crest on the gaping caldera's rim.

At the 0.3-mile mark, a snowfield lingers across the trail until August. Turn left at a junction just beyond the snow and climb 0.4 mile amid struggling mountain hemlock, white lupine, and patches of pinkish 5-petaled phlox. The summit tower, built in 1932, is staffed each summer with friendly rangers who help spot fires and answer hikers' questions. Soak in the view from the lookout's stone patio before heading back to your car.

If you'd like more exercise and different views, hike past your car to the north on a trail that climbs along a sandy ridge. This route skirts Hillman Peak for 2 miles, passing wildflower meadows, snow patches, rockfields with cat-sized marmots, and views across the Pumice Desert to the Three Sisters.

If you can't arrange to shuttle a car to the far end of the section—a lakeview pullout 2.2 miles from The Watchman's parking lot—turn back when the trail reaches a dramatic Crater Lake viewpoint beside the Devils Backbone. This craggy wall protruding from the lake's rim is a volcanic dike, formed when magma squeezed into a vertical crack inside ancient Mt. Mazama.

Hike 39

Cleetwood Cove

Closed in 2026 and 2027, the switchbacking trail down to Cleetwood Cove's tour boat dock is the most popular path in Crater Lake National Park.

Easy (to Cleetwood Cove)
2.2 miles round trip
700 feet elevation **loss**
Open late June to mid-October

Moderate (to Wizard Island summit)
4.5 miles round trip
1460 feet elevation gain
Open early July to early September

Phantom Ship.

This is also the only trail to Crater Lake's shore. Although the path down to the boat dock is "easy" by the standards of this book, the climb back up from the lakeshore can seem hot, steep, and difficult indeed if you are not used to hiking. Hikers who would like to explore the inside of Crater Lake's collapsed volcano more fully can take the boat tour and climb to Wizard Island's summit crater.

Pets are not allowed. Note that the Cleetwood Cove Trail will close after the summer of 2025 and will not reopen until July of 2028. In the meantime construction crews will rebuild the trail, stabilize cliffs to prevent dangerous rockfall, and add improved visitor facilities at the lakeshore, including new docks, expanded restrooms, and a new ticket office.

Getting There — From Crater Lake's Rim Village, take the Rim Drive clockwise 10.6 miles to the trailhead. If you're coming from the park's north entrance off Highway 138, turn left along the Rim Drive for 4.6 miles.

Rules for the boat tours are likely to change when the trail reopens in 2028. If it's 2025, first stop by the ticket office in the large parking lot across the road from the trailhead. Tickets can also be reserved at kiosks in Crater Lake Lodge and the Mazama Village gift shop within 24 hours of the boat departure, or at

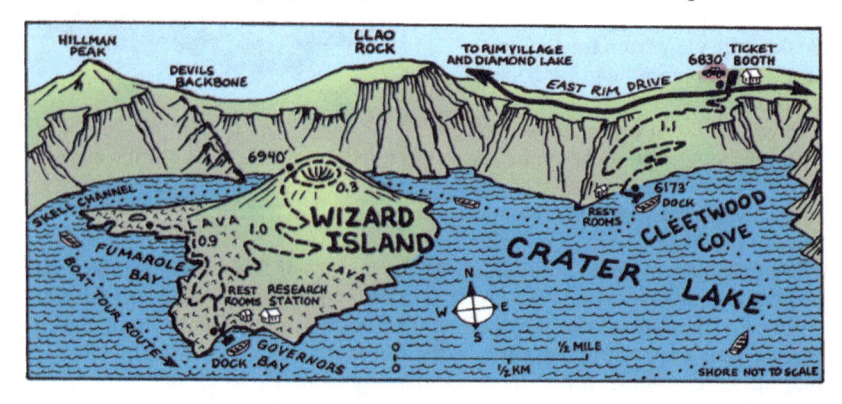

The Cleetwood Cove boat dock, with Wizard Island in the hazy distance.

explorecraterlake.com/things-to-do/boat-tours/ . But you'll still need to stop at the trailhead ticket office to pick them up.

Weather permitting, boats for the standard tour leave about six times a day from early July to early September. Tickets cost about $50 for adults or $35 for kids age 3-12. To make sure hikers don't miss their boat, sales for each tour stop 40 minutes before it leaves. Tour boats that also let you get out at Wizard Island cost a little more . Shuttle boats that only go to Wizard Island leave at 9am and 11:30am and cost a little less. Overnight stays on Wizard Island are not allowed.

The wide trail down to the boat dock passes lodgepole pines, Shasta red firs, mountain hemlocks, manzanita bushes, and lots of glimpses down to the glowing blue lake. The amazing color results from the lake's purity (it has no inlet other than precipitation) and its 1943-foot depth (it is the deepest lake in the U.S.). In recorded history the lake has only frozen twice and its surface level has fluctuated only 16 feet.

Gutsy swimmers sometimes brave the 50° F water at the dock's rocky shore.

Fishing has been permitted without a license ever since rangers realized that introduced trout and kokanee salmon are hurting the lake's biological balance.

The roofless tour boats carry up to 40 passengers and an interpretive ranger. It's a 45-minute ride to Wizard Island. The island is actually one of two cinder cones that erupted from the ruins of Mt. Mazama shortly after its cataclysmic collapse 7700 years ago. The other, Merriam Cone, was left under 486 feet of water after rain and melting snow gradually filled the lake. Wizard Island was named by Crater Lake's early promoter William Steel, who thought the cone resembled a sorcerer's hat. Although Steel helped win national park status, it's lucky some of his development schemes were ignored. He not only pushed for a rim road and a lodge, but also an aerial tramway from the rim to the island's top.

The trail on Wizard Island sets off through blocky black basalt lava colonized by golden-mantled ground squirrels, the pink blooms of bleeding hearts, and gnarled Shasta red firs. Take the trail's right fork to switchback up the cinder cone. At the top, a path circles the 90-foot-deep crater's rim amid storm-blasted pines, red paintbrush, and constant panoramas. On the way back down, don't miss the rocky 0.4-mile side trail to the house-sized lava boulders and emerald lakeshore at Fumarole Bay. A rougher path continues around the bay 0.5 mile.

The return boat trip passes the place where an unauthorized private helicopter crashed in 1995. It promptly sank with its passengers in 1500 feet of water and has never been recovered. The boat tour also circles Phantom Ship, a small craggy island that is actually a remnant of a 400,000-year-old volcanic plug—the oldest rock exposed on the lake. On the return trip, sharp-eyed passengers sometimes spot the Old Man of the Lake, a floating vertical log that's been roaming the lake for a century. Bring warm clothes for the sometimes chilly boat ride, and be sure to save energy for the 1.1-mile climb back to your car.

Hike 40 Mount Scott

Mt. Scott's lookout tower is the only place where hikers can fit the whole of Crater Lake into a single snapshot.

Moderate
5 miles round trip
1250 feet elevation gain
Open mid-July through October

Mt. Scott's summit.

Although Mt. Scott is a major mountain—tenth tallest in Oregon's Cascades—the trail is so well-graded that even families with children sometimes tackle it. Heavy winter snows make the Rim Drive near Mt. Scott the last road in Crater Lake National Park to open each summer. Pets are not allowed on the trail.

Getting There— If you're driving here from Medford or Klamath Falls on Highway 62, turn north past the park entrance booth 4 miles and turn right on

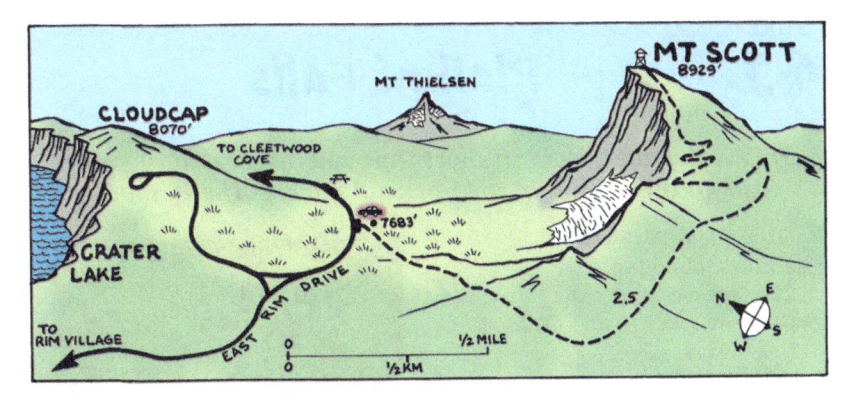

East Rim Drive for 11 miles to a parking pullout and trail sign on the right. If you're coming from Diamond Lake, turn left on East Rim Drive for 13 miles to the trailhead.

The trail begins as an ancient road track amid 5-needle whitebark pines and sparse meadows. Expect to cross a few snow patches until August. Also expect the company of Clark's nutcrackers, the gray-and-black cawing birds that tempt visitors to defy the park's ban on feeding wildlife. In fact, these "camp robbers" don't need handouts. Their sharp, strong beaks are adapted to break open whitebark pine cones for seeds, which they eat or cache for later. In return, the rugged whitebark pines, which only grow above 7000 feet, rely on the nutcrackers to spread their seeds from peak to peak.

The trail's second mile switchbacks up a slope of pumice pebbles, strewn like ochre hailstones from Mt. Mazama's fiery storm 7700 years ago. Views open up to the south across Klamath Lake's flats to the blue silhouette of the Mountain Lakes highland and the white tip of Mt. Shasta. To the right, Mt. McLoughlin's snowy cone rises above the summits of the Sky Lakes Wilderness. Wildflowers along the way include red paintbrush, purple penstemon, and the fuzzy seed stalks of western pasque flower.

At the summit you'll find a locked, two-story stone-and-frame lookout. Built in 1953, the lookout replaced a similar stone cabin from the 1920s. To the north, look for Mt. Thielsen's spire and the distant Three Sisters. Mt. Scott's name honors Levi Scott, an 1844 Oregon Trail pioneer who founded Douglas County's Scottsburg and helped scout the Applegate Trail to Southern Oregon.

Crater Lake from Mt. Scott.

Hike 41 — Plaikni Falls

This waterfall hike is so short that you might add the other walk in this corner of the national park — The Pinnacles.

Easy (Plaikni Falls)
2 miles round trip
200 feet elevation gain
Open mid-July to mid-October
Use: hikers

Easy (The Pinnacles)
1 mile round trip
50 feet elevation gain
Use: hikers, bicycles

The one-mile packed gravel path to Plaikni Falls ends in a wildflower glen with a spring-fed cascade. At The Pinnacles, you can stroll half a mile along the rim of a canyon of weird ash spires to discover an abandoned park entrance.

Getting There — From Park Headquarters (halfway between Rim Village and Highway 62), drive 0.1 mile south toward Highway 62 and fork to the left on East Rim Drive for 8.5 miles. Just before the Phantom Ship Overlook at Kerr Notch, turn right on Pinnacles Road. After a mile down this paved road, park at the Plaikni Falls pullout on the left. Pets are banned.

The path sets off across Kerr Valley, a flat-bottomed canyon carved by one of the glaciers that descended the flanks of Mt. Mazama in the Ice Age. When Mt. Mazama erupted and collapsed to create Crater Lake about 7700 years ago, the valley was amputated, leaving Kerr Notch as a U-shaped dip in the caldera rim.

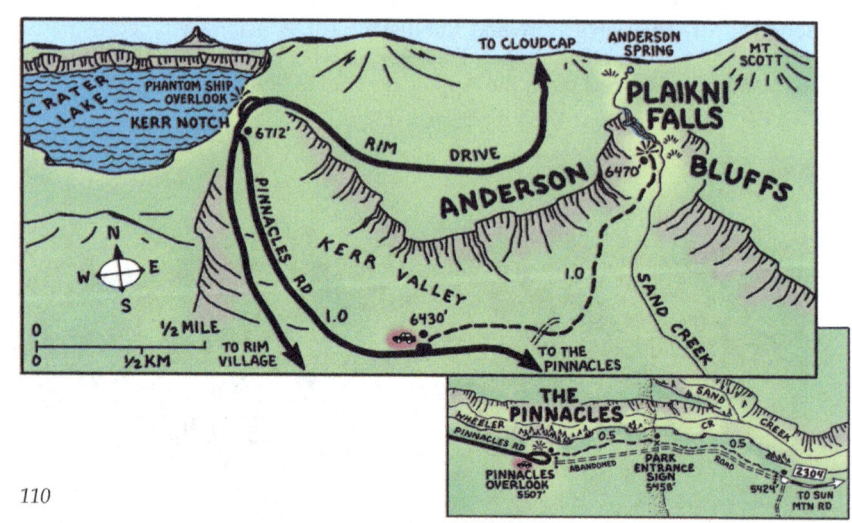

As Mt. Mazama collapsed, a glowing avalanche of superheated rock and ash raced down Kerr Valley. Since then, Shasta red fir and mountain hemlock have managed to reforest the valley. Because of the deep winter snow and pumice soil at this elevation, there is virtually no underbrush.

After 0.3 mile the trail crosses an abandoned roadbed, part of an old fire road to the park's eastern border. In the 1930s, this road was used to access a large quarry that extended to the left of the trail as far as Anderson Bluffs. Workers from the Civilian Conservation Corps (CCC) quarried rock from the cliffs to build viewpoint walkways and walls along Rim Drive.

The trail skirts the base of Anderson Bluffs and suddenly emerges from the woods at a meadow along Sand Creek. A few hundred feet later the trail ends at a rock-walled patio with a view of a 20-foot waterfall. Asked to choose a name for the cascade, the Klamath tribe picked *plaikni*, a Klamath word for waters from Crater Lake's high country.

Columbine.

Wildflowers crowding the brook here include blue lupine, pink monkeyflower, red paintbrush, columbine, and purple monkshood. To protect this fragile area, please don't leave the trail. Return as you came.

To find the trailhead for The Pinnacles, drive south on paved Pinnacles Road another 6 miles to a turnaround at road's end. The pinnacles here are a remnant of the ash flow that filled the canyons of Wheeler Creek and Sand Creek 7700 years ago. Superheated gas continued to vent up through the ash for months, welding it into pillars of solid rock. Since then the creeks have eroded away most of the loose ash, exposing the hardened vents as spires.

Mt. Scott from The Pinnacles.

After admiring the view from the turnaround, take the trail to the right along the canyon rim. The forest here is almost entirely lodgepole pine, one of the few trees that can survive in such dry, sandy soil. At the half-mile mark you'll reach a stone monument with the park's old entrance sign. Most hikers turn back here, although a fainter path with fewer views continues another half mile to a rarely used gravel turnaround at the end of Forest Service Road 2304.

Hike 42 — Sun Notch

What's the difference between a caldera and a crater? To find out, visit two uncrowded paths on the south side of Crater Lake—a stroll to Sun Notch and a hike to Crater Peak.

Easy (to Sun Notch)
0.5-mile loop
115 feet elevation gain
Open July to early November

Moderate (to Crater Peak)
6.8 miles round trip
1010 feet elevation gain

Phantom Ship from Sun Notch.

The short Sun Notch Trail climbs to a spectacular Crater Lake viewpoint above Phantom Ship's craggy little island. But the astonishingly blue, 6-mile-wide lake you see here is not in a crater at all—it fills a *caldera*, a giant pit created by a mountain's collapse. To see a true volcanic crater, take the nearby 3.2-mile path to Crater Peak, a cinder cone with a wildflower meadow in a cute little summit bowl. Pets are not allowed on either trail.

Getting There— Start at the national park headquarters and visitor information building located halfway between Crater Lake's Rim Village and Highway 62. Drive 0.1 mile down the road toward Highway 62, turn left at a "Rim Drive (East)" sign, and follow this road 4.3 miles to the Sun Notch Trailhead on the left. Then hike the short path up through mountain hemlock woods to the cliff-edge viewpoint.

Much of Crater Lake's geologic story is exposed at Sun Notch's viewpoint. When eruptions started building Mt. Mazama 400,000 years ago, they began near here. Phantom Ship is a fragment of the volcanic plug from those early eruptions. As Mt. Mazama grew to an estimated height of 12,000 feet, the volcanic vents moved farther north, finally pouring out a thick dacite flow to create Llao Rock, the largest cliff visible across the lake. By then, glaciers were scouring deep

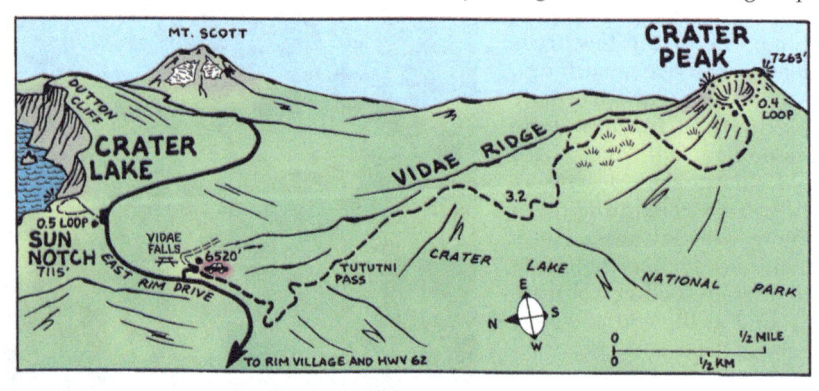

The view of Crater Lake's caldera from Sun Notch.

U-shaped valleys into the mountain's flanks. Sun Notch is a remnant of one of the largest of these glacial troughs, amputated when the mountain exploded 7700 years ago.

If you'd like to see a genuine crater after visiting Sun Notch, drive 1.4 miles back on Rim Drive and turn left down to the Vidae Falls Picnic Area. Park here and hike the Crater Peak Trail, which traverses a slope below Rim Drive for 0.6 mile. Then the path strikes off along a broad ridge through mountain hemlock woods with patches of blue lupine, scarlet gilia, and golden currant bushes. After 2.1 mostly level miles the path climbs 0.5 mile to the mouth of the summit crater. Pumice and ash that rained down from Mt. Mazama's eruption filled this little crater halfway to the top. Since then lupine, dogbane, and grass have colonized the bowl, making it a popular grazing spot for elk; look for their hoofprints and sign. A patch of snow lingers in the crater until August.

For a view-packed 0.4-mile loop, walk clockwise around Crater Peak's rim. To the north, note Mt. Thielsen's distant spire above Sun Notch. To the east is Mt. Scott; to the west is Union Peak's spire; and to the south are Klamath Lake, distant Mt. Shasta, and snowy Mt. McLoughlin.

Lupine in Crater Peak's summit meadow.

Hike 43
Union Peak

> The oldest mountain in Crater Lake National Park, Union Peak's rocky volcanic plug has views from Mt. Thielsen to Mt. Shasta.

Difficult
11 miles round trip
1600 feet elevation gain
Open mid-July through October

Union Peak from the trail.

    The panorama comes with a price, however—the hike's first 2.9 miles are a long march through the woods, while the final 0.8 mile is a steep climb up three dozen rocky switchbacks. The summit view encompasses the forested flanks of Crater Lake, but not the lake itself. A few other cautions: backpackers must pick up an overnight permit at a national park office, pets are not permitted, and there is no water.

    Getting There— Start by driving 72 miles east of Medford (or 1 mile west of Crater Lake National Park's south entrance) to the summit of Highway 62. At a "Pacific Crest Trail Parking" sign, turn south to a dirt turnaround. The nearly level trail sets off through a sparse forest that alternates between stands of almost pure lodgepole pine and groves of almost pure mountain hemlock. The pumice that fell here 10 feet deep during the eruption of Crater Lake's Mt. Mazama 7700 years ago is responsible for the utter lack of underbrush.

    In a pumice plain at the 2.9-mile mark, turn right at a sign for the Union Peak Trail and gain a first glimpse of Union Peak ahead. The path now climbs gradually through meadow openings with blue lupine and lots of elk sign. Once hunted nearly to extinction, elk were restocked here from Yellowstone National Park in the 1960s and are thriving.

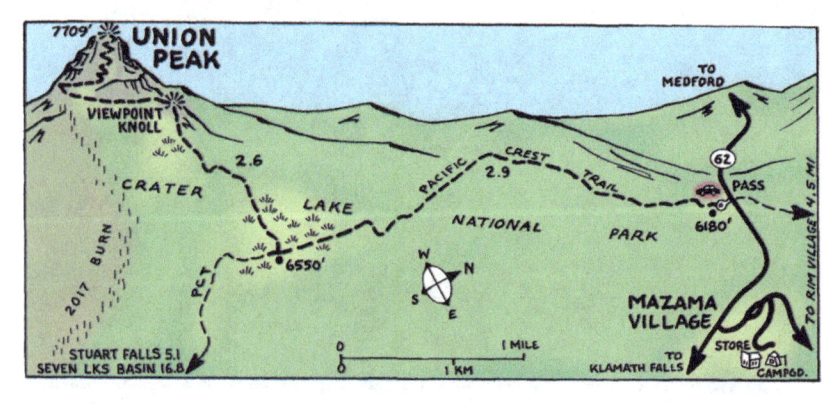

After a mile the trail crests a knoll with the hike's first sweeping views. The path follows this scenic ridge, traverses left across a huge rockslide, switchbacks to recross the slide, and then launches up Union Peak—a gigantic rockpile surmounted with a fortress of black crags.

As you switchback up, look for the dishmop-shaped seedheads of western pasque flower and the purple trumpets of penstemon. The final short switchbacks are so rugged you may need to use your hands as you climb.

The summit's black boulders have shiny spots of melted rock where lightning has struck, proving this is no place to be in a storm. On a clear day, however, distant Mt. Shasta floats ghost-like on the southern horizon above Devils Peak, with the cone of Mt. McLoughlin to the right.

The seedheads of Pasque flower ("hippie plant").

To the west is the Rogue Valley's haze. To the north, it's easy to imagine Mt. Mazama's former shape, although the mountain's forested flanks now rise to a broken hole. Crater Lake itself is hidden inside but Llao Rock's cliff, on the lake's far shore, peeks out above Rim Village.

Crater Lake's rim from Union Peak's summit.

115

Southern Cascades

Mt. McLoughlin from Lake of the Woods (Hike #50).

The High Lakes Trail (Hike #50).

Trapper and Margurette Lakes in the Sky Lakes Basin (Hike #47).

The Pacific Crest Trail on Brown Mountainn (Hike #49).

Hike 44 — Seven Lakes Basin

From Devils Peak's summit the pools of the forested Seven Lakes Basin look like pips on a pair of green dice.

Moderate (to Alta Lake)
8.4 miles round trip
1750 feet elevation gain
Open early July through October
Use: hikers, horses

Difficult (to Cliff Lake)
10.4 miles round trip
2300 feet elevation gain

Difficult (to Devils Peak)
13.7-mile loop
3050 feet elevation gain

Alta Lake.

Up close, each of the seven lakes has its own character. Half-mile-long Alta Lake, for example, is so narrow you can throw a rock across it. Cliff Lake has a mountain view and a diving rock popular with swimmers.

The Seven Lakes Trail is the shortest route to this popular basin, but it climbs across a high ridge. Be warned that mosquitoes are a problem from mid-July to mid-August. Group size is limited to eight people and 12 animals. Backpackers must tent at least 100 feet from lakeshores and are encouraged to use the four signed camp areas. Equestrians are required to use the eight designated horse camps. In addition, horses are not allowed within 200 feet of lakeshores (except on trails or at designated watering spots) and grazing is usually banned.

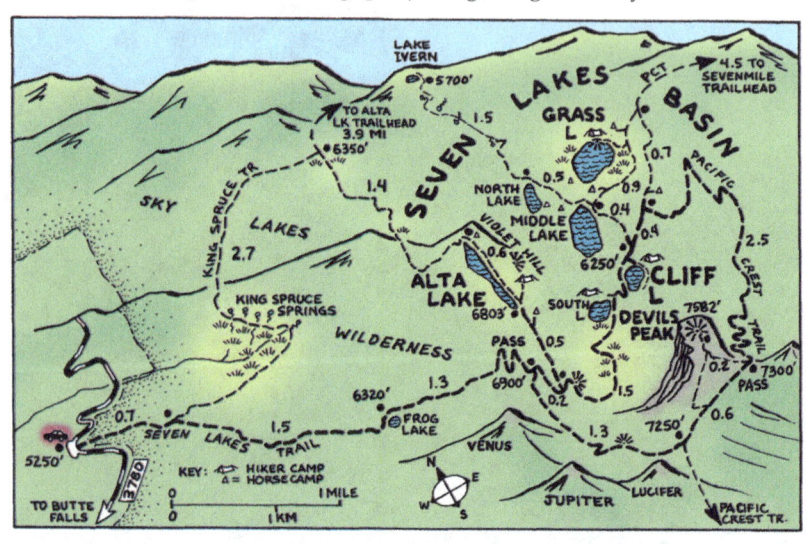

Getting There — Take Highway 62 east from Medford 14.5 miles, turn right on the Butte Falls Highway for 15 miles to the town of Butte Falls, continue straight for another 1 mile, turn left at a sign for Prospect for 9 miles, turn right onto Lodgepole Road 34 for 8.5 miles, continue straight on Road 37 for 0.4 mile, and then veer right onto gravel Road 3780 for 4.1 miles.

The trail starts behind a guardrail and climbs steadily up a broad forested ridge. The path is a bit dusty and rocky from heavy use by horses and hikers, especially on summer weekends. Fork to the right at the 0.7-mile mark, and after another 1.5 miles take a break beside Frog Lake, a shallow pool rimmed with heather and lodgepole pine. Then continue 1.3 miles to a pass with a trail junction and a view ahead to Devils Peak. The thumb-shaped outcrop on the peak's left shoulder is the old volcano's original plug, stripped bare by the vanished Ice Age glacier that carved the lake basin below.

Go straight down the far side of the pass 0.2 mile to a second trail junction — this one for Alta Lake. For a moderate hike, turn left half a mile to this amazingly straight, skinny pool, aligned on the crack of a major north-south fault. Before turning back, be sure to follow a "Camping" pointer right 300 feet to the cliffy lip of Violet Hill and a view across the Seven Lakes Basin.

Devils Peak from Grass Lake.

If you're up to a more difficult hike, skip the Alta Lake side trail and continue straight 1.5 miles to Cliff Lake. Along the way you'll descend through subalpine meadows with the tiny blooms of pink heather and white partridge foot. Pause at the rockslide between South Lake and Cliff Lake to watch for pikas, the round-eared "rock rabbits" that *meep!* at passing hikers.

If you're backpacking, or if you can manage an even longer day hike, continue on a spectacular loop to Devils Peak. Go straight past Cliff Lake 0.4 mile, turn right on the Pacific Crest Trail, take this well-graded route 2.5 miles to a pass, and turn right on an unmarked path up a rocky ridge 0.2 mile to Devils Peak's summit. The panorama here spins from Mt. Thielsen and the Crater Lake rim to Klamath Lake and Mt. McLoughlin's snowy cone. On the way down, keep right at trail junctions for 1.9 view-packed miles. Then turn left on the Seven Lakes Trail for 3.5 miles to your car.

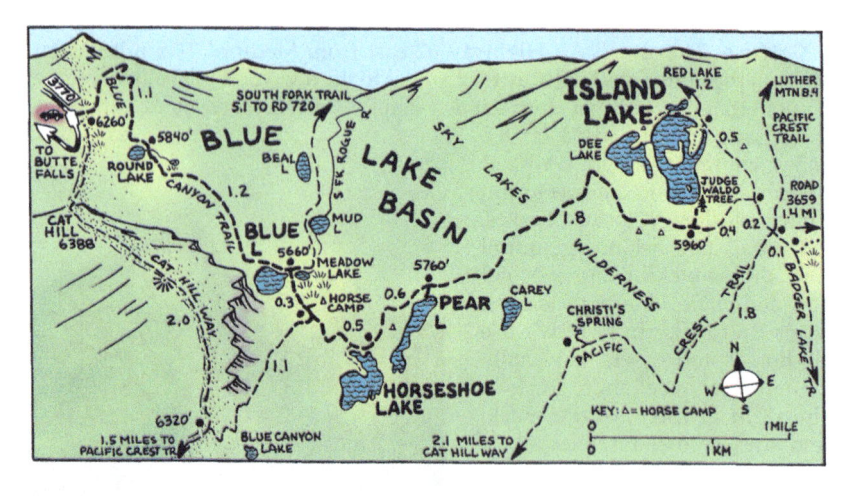

Hike
45 Blue Lake Basin

This corner of the Sky Lakes Wilderness has been popular since at least 1888, when Judge John Waldo camped here.

Easy (to Blue Lake)
4.6 miles round trip
640 feet elevation gain
Open early July through October
Use: hikers, horses

Moderate (to Horseshoe Lake)
6.2 miles round trip
700 feet elevation gain

Difficult (to Island Lake)
11 miles round trip
1300 feet elevation gain
6.1-mile loop

The Waldo Tree at Island Lake.

Waldo led a party of five Salem horsemen from Willamette Pass to Mt. Shasta in 1888, becoming the first to trace the route of the present-day Pacific Crest Trail through Southern Oregon. At Island Lake, Waldo's group carved their names in a large Shasta red fir. Today hikers who trek 5.5 miles along the Blue Canyon Trail can still read the inscription. But it's tempting to turn back at one of the smaller, prettier lakes along the way.

The area's popularity has brought a few rules. Maximum group size is eight people and 12 animals. Backpackers must tent at least 100 feet from lakeshores. Equestrians are required to use designated horse camps. Horses are not allowed within 200 feet of lakeshores or 50 feet of streams (except on trails or at designated watering spots) and grazing is usually banned. Also remember that mosquitoes are a problem from mid-July to mid-August.

Island Lake. Below: Mt. McLoughlin from Island Lake.

Getting There— Drive Highway 62 east from Medford 14.5 miles, turn right on the Butte Falls Highway for 15 miles to the town of Butte Falls, continue straight for another 1 mile, turn left at a sign for Prospect for 9 miles, turn right onto Lodgepole Road 34 for 8.5 miles, turn right on Road 37 for 5.3 miles of pavement and an additional 2.1 miles of gravel, and finally turn left on gravel Road 3770 for 5.3 miles to a large parking pullout on the right.

The trail heads downhill into a forest of Shasta red fir with blue lupine blooms in late July and ripe blue huckleberries in late August. After 1.1 mile the path passes Round Lake—a scenic pool, but no match for Blue Lake, another 1.2 miles down the trail. Backed by a rockslide from a dramatic 300-foot cliff, Blue Lake is filled with deep green water suitable for swimming. From the mountain hemlock woods along the shore, you can watch dragonflies zoom or listen to the *meep!* of pikas scampering about the rockslide.

Hikers with children may want to turn back here. To continue, however, turn right at a trail junction near Blue Lake's outlet and then go straight 0.8 mile to Horseshoe Lake. The trail only touches the small end of this lopsided horseshoe. To find the prettier end, backtrack 300 feet on the trail and take a side path out to the lake's peninsula— off-limits to tenters, of course.

If you're headed for more distant lakes, note that neither Pear Lake nor Island Lake is visible from the main trail. Beyond Horseshoe Lake 0.6 mile, look for a short spur on the right that leads to Pear Lake, obviously named before bananas were common. Another 1.8 miles along the main trail, a large unmarked fork leads 0.1 mile to Judge Waldo's railed tree and the only grassy bank along the shore of large, brush-rimmed Island Lake.

Hike 46　Mount McLoughlin

Mt. McLoughlin overlooks half the state, and a good share of California too. The trail to the top is tough, but not technical.

Very difficult
10.6 miles round trip
3915 feet elevation gain
Open July through October

Mt. McLoughlin from the air.

For years there was no official trail to the summit, so climbers spread out on a maze of scramble paths, spray-painting dots on rocks to help them find the route back. In the mid-1990s Forest Service crews laid out a single clear route and chipped away the ugly, misleading markings. The hike is still one of the most demanding — and rewarding — in Southern Oregon. Only set out in good weather, bring sunscreen, and carry plenty of water. Maximum group size is eight.

From a distance, Mt. McLoughlin's relatively smooth cone suggests it is one of the youngest Cascade volcanoes. Climbers, however, can see massive gouges left by Ice Age glaciers on the peak's hidden north face, exposing a thumb-shaped lava plug. The most recent eruption, 12,000 years ago, poured blocky basalt from a vent low on the mountain's south slope.

The tallest peak in Southern Oregon has had many names. Klamath Indians called it *Kesh yainatat*, home of the dwarf old woman who commanded the west wind. The Takelma tribe dubbed it *Alwilamchaildis* after a mythic hero of their legends, and thought it was the home of Acorn Woman, who made oaks bear fruit each year. In 1838, the first map to show the peak labeled it Mt. McLoughlin in honor of the Hudson's Bay Company leader at Fort Vancouver. After Rogue Valley settlers began calling the peak Mt. Pitt (for California's Pit River), the Oregon legislature resolved in 1905 to restore the McLoughlin name.

Getting There — From Medford, take Highway 62 east 6 miles and turn right toward Klamath Falls on Highway 140 for 36 miles. Between mileposts

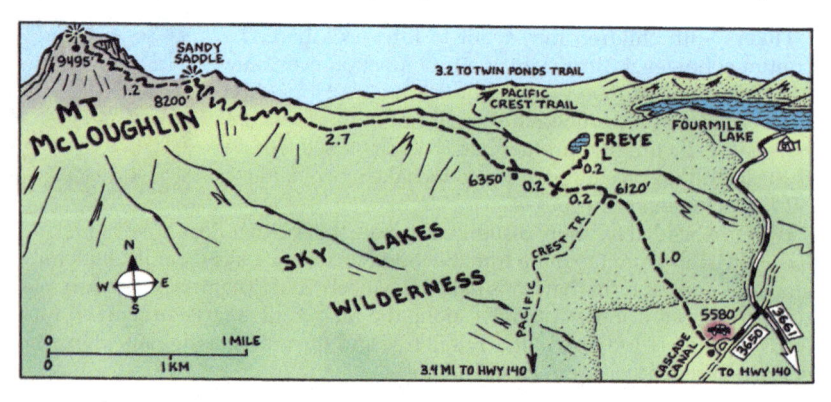

The final pitch to the summit.   Below: The view of Fourmile Lake from the top.

35 and 36, turn left at a "Fourmile Lake" pointer onto gravel Road 3661 for 2.9 miles, and then turn left on Road 3650 for 0.2 mile to a large parking lot. (From Klamath Falls, take Highway 140 west to just beyond milepost 36, turn right on Road 3661 for 2.9 miles, and turn left on Road 3650.)

The trail promptly crosses Cascade Canal, which shunts Fourmile Lake's outlet stream west toward Rogue Valley irrigators. Then the path marches steadily up through a mixed forest of Shasta red fir. After a mile, veer right onto the Pacific Crest Trail. In another 0.2 mile, an unmarked spur to the right leads over a rise to Freye Lake, a shallow pool with a view of the mountain's top half. To continue your climb, return to the PCT, follow it a few hundred feet uphill, and fork left on the Mt. McLoughlin Trail.

The next 1.5 miles are relatively easy, through boulder-strewn mountain hemlock woods. But then the route launches uphill with a vengeance to timberline, where only pinemat manzanita and gnarled whitebark pines survive. At the 4.1-mile mark the trail clambers to a sandy saddle where the sweeping view includes your first glimpse of Mt. McLoughlin's true summit. The final 1.2 miles gain a staggering 1300 feet along a craggy ridgecrest.

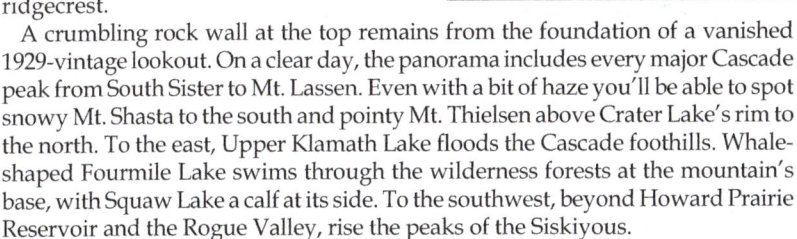

A crumbling rock wall at the top remains from the foundation of a vanished 1929-vintage lookout. On a clear day, the panorama includes every major Cascade peak from South Sister to Mt. Lassen. Even with a bit of haze you'll be able to spot snowy Mt. Shasta to the south and pointy Mt. Thielsen above Crater Lake's rim to the north. To the east, Upper Klamath Lake floods the Cascade foothills. Whale-shaped Fourmile Lake swims through the wilderness forests at the mountain's base, with Squaw Lake a calf at its side. To the southwest, beyond Howard Prairie Reservoir and the Rogue Valley, rise the peaks of the Siskiyous.

When you hike down, stick to the ridgecrest trail you followed on the way up. Don't be tempted to romp down a snowfield (or by August, a scree slope) to the right of the ridge. Nearly every year, search parties are organized for hikers lured far south of the trail by this "shortcut."

Hike 30
Sky Lakes Basin

The easiest route into the lake-dotted high country of the Sky Lakes Wilderness, this loop passes half a dozen lakes.

Easy
6.9-mile loop
400 feet elevation gain
Open early July through October
Use: hikers, horses

Fireweed

The beautiful Sky Lakes Basin also has downsides: you can expect crowds on summer weekends, mosquitoes are a nuisance from mid-July to mid-August, and the first two miles of the hike burned in a 2017 forest fire. Maximum group size is eight people and 12 animals.

Getting There — Drive east of Medford 6 miles on Highway 62, turn right on Highway 140 toward Klamath Falls to milepost 41, and turn left at a "Cold Springs Trailhead" pointer onto Road 3651. Follow this gravel road 10.1 miles to its end at a turnaround with a primitive campground and a restored, shake-sided shelter beside a cold, piped spring. (If you're coming from Klamath Falls, take Highway 140 west to milepost 41 and turn right on Road 3651.)

The broad, dusty trail sets off through an area that burned in 2017. Expect pink fireweed, pearly everlasting, and views of Mt. McLoughlin.

After 0.6 mile the trail forks. Both paths pass another mile of black snags before reaching unburned woods at the lake basin, but the right-hand fork gets there a bit quicker, so branch right on the South Rock Creek Trail. In another 1.8 miles you'll reach a delightful isthmus between the Heavenly Twin Lakes.

This is a great place to let kids explore the shores of these shallow lakes, and it offers a rare glimpse of Luther Mountain and Devils Peak at the far northern end of the Sky Lakes Basin. Red and blue huckleberries ripen in August. If you're

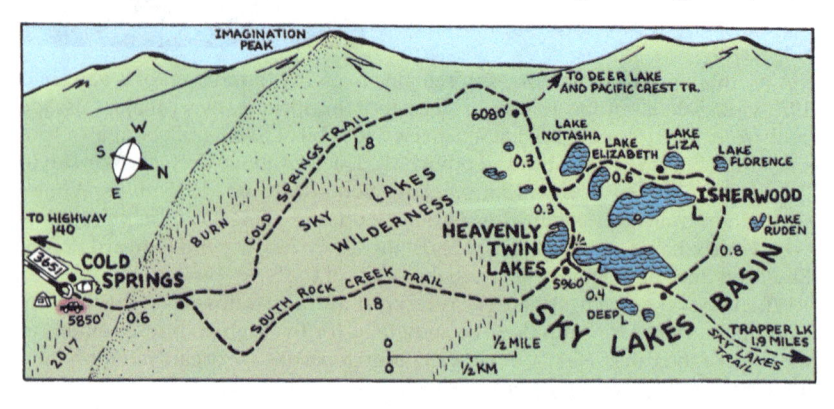

Red huckleberries are just as edible as blue huckleberries.

backpacking, remember that camping is banned within 100 feet of lakeshores, so this isthmus is off limits.

When you're ready to continue the loop, backtrack from the isthmus and veer left along the shore of the larger Heavenly Twin for 0.4 mile. At the far end of this lake, turn left on the Isherwood Trail for 0.8 mile to reach the shore of dramatic, half-mile-long Isherwood Lake. The smooth, curved bedrock shore was polished by glaciers that capped the Cascade Range during the Ice Age. Look closely for scratch marks showing the direction the ice flowed as it slowly carved the Sky Lakes Basin. Then continue along the trail 0.6 mile, passing lima-bean-shaped Lake Elizabeth and deep, blue-green Lake Notasha.

At a junction just beyond Lake Notasha, turn right for 0.3 mile. Then complete the loop by forking left onto the Cold Springs Trail for the final 2.4-mile walk back to your car.

Other Options — Backpackers can continue north from the Heavenly Twin Lakes for 1.9 miles to Trapper Lake, and from there explore a different part of the long Sky Lakes Basin.

Isherwood Lake.

Hike 48

Fish Lake

A bicycle-friendly trail links Fish Lake with Lake of the Woods, passing the lava flows of the Cascade summit on the way.

Easy (to Fish Lake Resort)
6.6 miles round trip
100 feet elevation gain
Open mid-May to mid-November
Use: hikers, bicycles

Moderate (High Lakes Trail)
9.3 miles one way
500 feet elevation gain

Brown Mountain from Fish Lake.

The lakes on either end of the broad High Lakes Trail are probably Southern Oregon's most popular—each has campgrounds, picnic areas, boat launches, and a rustic, old-timey resort. If the 9.3-mile, packed-gravel High Lakes Trail sounds too long, try the ungraveled 3.3-mile trail along Fish Lake's shore instead. Because the two trails connect end-to-end, adventurous hikers (or bicyclists) can do them both.

Getting There— The Fish Lake Trail is easy enough for hikers with children. To find it, drive Highway 140 east of Medford 35 miles (or west of Klamath Falls 40 miles). Between mileposts 28 and 29, turn south on paved Road 37 at a "North Fork Campground" pointer. After half a mile turn left into the trailhead parking pullout, just opposite the campground entrance.

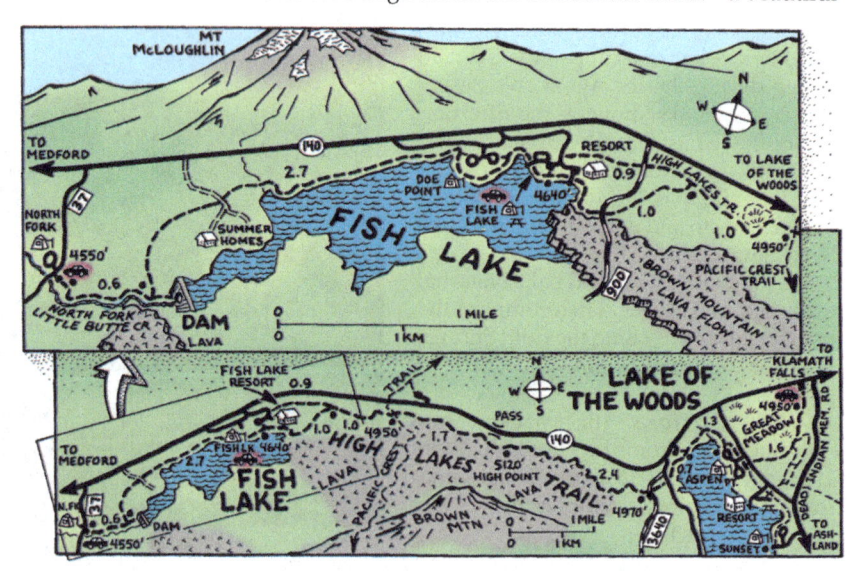

The Fish Lake Trail sets off along North Fork Little Butte Creek—a beautiful stream that begins as a glassy, meandering, meadow-edged river but soon shifts to a rushing whitewater torrent. Fir trees grow 4 feet thick along the path, with an understory of hazel and a few wildflowers. Look for white, 3-petaled trillium, fuzzy pink spirea, and lavender lousewort.

At a trail junction after 0.6 mile, the main trail turns left away from the creek, but a spur continues straight 300 feet to the base of Fish Lake's dam. Arduously built in 1921-22 by men hauling rocks in horse-drawn railroad cars, the dam tripled Fish Lake's size. The original lake was created a few thousand years ago by a natural rock dam — the Brown Mountain lava flow visible across the creek. The Medford Irrigation District draws down the enlarged reservoir each summer to water orchards.

After leaving the creek, the Fish Lake Trail makes a tedious 0.8-mile detour to avoid private summer homes. But then the path sticks to the lakeshore for 1.9 miles, skirting two campgrounds and a picnic area before reaching the Fish Lake Resort. The dock, cafe, and general store here make a good turnaround point.

Want a longer hike? If you're planning to hike (or bicycle) the High Lakes Trail from Fish Lake to Lake of the Woods, it's probably best to start at the Fish Lake Campground. To find this trailhead, drive Highway 140 east of Medford 35 miles (or west of Klamath Falls 38 miles). Between mileposts 30 and 31, turn south at a "Fish Lake Recreation Area" sign and keep left for 0.4 mile to the start of the High Lakes Trail on the left. There's no room for parking here, however, and the nearby Fish Lake Resort has no parking for trail users either, so you'll have to drive on 300 feet to the Fish Lake Campground and pay a $5 day-use parking fee. Then walk (or ride your bike) back to the trail.

From Fish Lake, the well-graded, 8-foot-wide High Lakes Trail climbs through ancient lava flows that have grown over with forest. The trail is often within 300 feet of noisy Highway 140. At the 1.8-mile the path skirts a sinkhole where water from the 20-foot-wide Cascade Canal vanishes underground. Irrigators built the canal to shunt Fourmile Lake's outlet creek toward the Fish Lake reservoir. To their chagrin, the canal's water vanished into a lava tube here. Then they realized the tube carries the water underground to Fish Lake anyway.

North Fork Little Butte Creek.

Just beyond the sinkhole, the path crosses the Pacific Crest Trail (closed to bikes; see Hike #49). Then the High Lakes Trail climbs another 1.7 miles along the edge of a fresh-looking lava flow to the Cascade summit and descends 3.1 miles to the shore of Lake of the Woods. If you continue 1.3 miles, you'll cross two bridges at the marshy end of the lake (with views, ducks, and mosquitoes) before reaching a trail junction at Aspen Point's north picnic area. A fee is charged if you park a car here. If you keep left at trail junctions and cross two roads, however, you'll follow the High Lakes Trail 1.6 miles around a vast, grassy plain to trail's end at the Great Meadow Recreation Site. To bring a shuttle car to this free parking lot, drive Highway 140 to between mileposts 37 and 38.

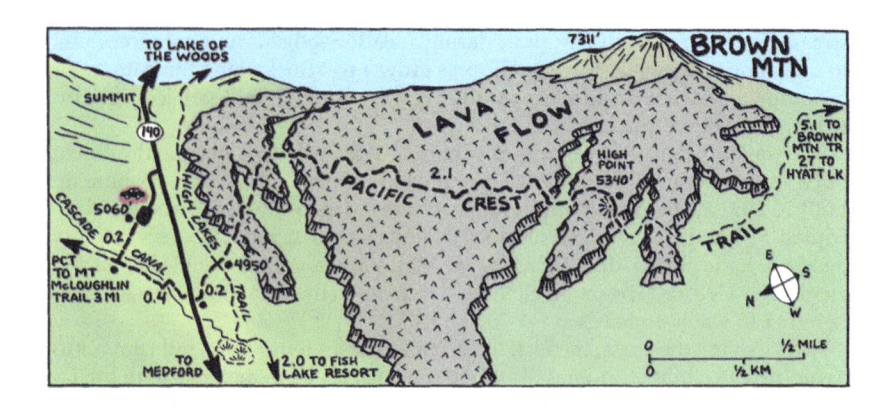

Hike 49 Brown Mountain Lava

The lava flows on Brown Mountain are so rugged that trail builders had to dynamite the surface to lay a tread.

Easy (to view at high point)
5.8-mile loop
550 feet elevation gain
Open June to mid-November
Use: hikers, horses

Chinkapin "porcupine eggs".

Perhaps the most expensive portion of the 2400-mile Pacific Crest Trail, this spectacular pathway of crushed red cinders through jumbled basalt is now easy to hike. From Highway 140, the path climbs gently to viewpoints of Brown Mountain, Fish Lake, and Mt. McLoughlin.

Getting There — From Medford, take Highway 62 east 6 miles and turn right toward Klamath Falls on Highway 140 to the Cascade crest. Between mileposts 32 and 33, turn north at a "Summit Sno-Park" sign and drive to the far end of the huge paved parking area.

The trail that starts here crosses a grassy, open fir forest for 0.2 mile and crosses a footbridge to the Pacific Crest Trail. Turn left, following the canal 0.4 mile to a crossing of noisy Highway 140. Of course you could start your hike at this unmarked crossing (Highway 140 does offer a small parking pullout at the end of a guardrail by milepost 32), but the walk alongside Cascade Canal can be quite pleasant. The canal was built to divert Fourmile Lake's outlet to the west side of the Cascade summit for Medford irrigators. When full, the rushing 20-foot creek provides a stark contrast to the lava ahead.

Beyond the highway crossing 0.2 mile, the PCT crosses the packed-gravel High Lakes Trail (see Hike #48). Shortly afterward, the PCT enters a moonscape of black boulders, with views ahead to Brown Mountain, the lava's source. Brown Mountain is called a shield volcano because of its low profile, built up by countless flows of runny black lava. About 2000 years ago a cinder cone erupted on the summit, adding a brown peak with a little crater. Shortly afterward, the lava you're crossing vented from the cinder cone's base. The flow's crust cooled first and jumbled when the lava underneath kept moving.

A surprising variety of life has gained a foothold here. Where the rocks aren't disturbed, they're crusted with gray, green, and black lichens—a combination of fungus and algae that gets all the nutrients it needs from the rain and the air. Another pioneer, chinkapin, forms 10-foot-tall bushes along the trail, with sprays of white flowers in summer and spiny fruit (known as "porcupine eggs") in the fall. Some animals live in lava to escape predators. Watch for orange-bellied Douglas squirrels and listen for the *meep!* of guinea-pig-shaped pikas.

At the 2.9-mile mark, by a cairn with the last best view of Mt. McLoughlin's huge cone, the PCT reaches a high point and begins heading downhill through Douglas fir woods. This makes a good turnaround point, although long-distance hikers can continue 5.7 miles to the Brown Mountain Trail crossing, 7.6 miles to a spring at the South Brown Mountain Shelter, or 9.6 miles to a parking area near milepost 27 of Dead Indian Memorial Road.

Mt. McLoughlin from the lava flow.

Hike 50 — Lake of the Woods

Reflecting Mt. McLoughlin's snowy pyramid, this lake is one of the most popular destinations in the Southern Cascades.

Moderate
7.1-mile loop
No elevation gain
Open June to mid-November
Use: hikers, horses, bicycles

Mt. McLoughlin from the lake.

Lake of the Woods has campgrounds, a rustic resort, ramps for ski boats, giant meadows, bird-filled marshes, and lots of easy trails. The 7.1-mile exploration suggested here hits the highlights, but there are plenty of shorter options too.

For the best view of Mt. McLoughlin, start at the Sunset boat ramp. If you aren't staying at the resort or a campground, expect to pay $5 to park here, and anywhere else at this end of the lake. Note that mosquitoes are a problem from late June to late July.

Getting There — From Ashland, drive Interstate 5 to south Ashland exit 14, head east on Highway 66 for 0.7 mile, and turn left on Dead Indian Memorial Road for 34 miles. At milepost 34, turn left on the Sunset Boat Launch entry road. If you're coming from Medford, it's quicker to drive Highway 140 east 44 miles, turn right at a "Lake of the Woods Resort" sign for 1.3 miles, and turn right on Dead Indian Memorial Road for 0.9 mile. If you're coming from

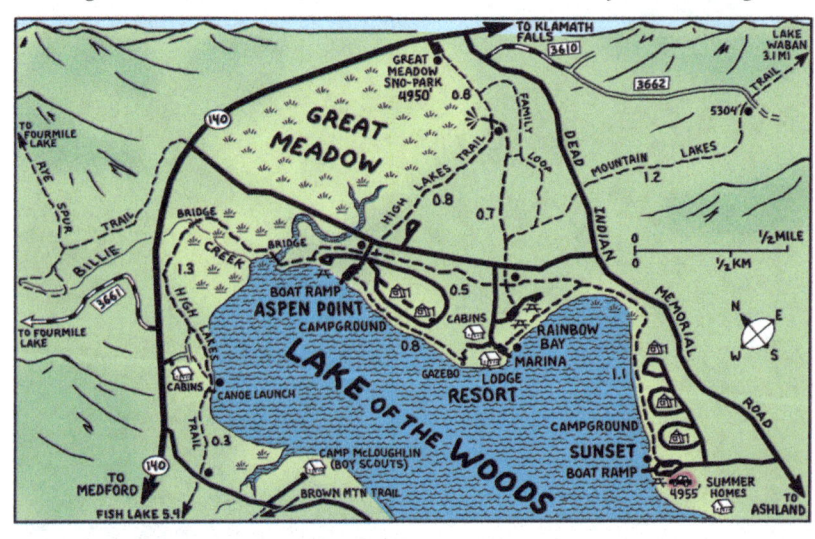

130

Klamath Falls, take Highway 140 west 32 miles, and turn left on Dead Indian Memorial Road for 2.4 miles.

Start at a "Sunset Trail" sign on the right-hand side of the boat launch loop and follow this braided path north along the lakeshore through shady Douglas fir woods. For the first half mile you'll pass campground sites (on your right) and small, swimmable gravel beaches (on your left). Then the path skirts the marshy end of Rainbow Bay and comes to a large, unsigned fork.

The Sunset Trail goes straight, and it's a better route if you're biking, but if you're on foot it's more fun to fork left, continuing along the lakeshore through a big picnic area 0.3 mile to the resort's marina. Continue 200 feet to find the resort's general store and lodge. The lodge's restaurant has a great patio.

To the right of the lodge, briefly follow a road between rental cabins and then take a trail that switchbacks down to a lakefront gazebo. From here the lakeshore path continues north, skirting campsites another half mile to the huge, paved Aspen Point Boat Launch.

Turn right, following the entrance road 200 feet to a fee booth. The wide, packed gravel High Lakes Trail crosses the road here. If you're tired, you could simply turn right and follow "Sunset Trail" signs 1.6 miles back to your car.

Above: The High Lakes Trail.
Below: Great Meadow.

If you'd like to see more of the lake, however, turn left on the High Lakes Trail. This bike path skirts a picnic area and then crosses a bridge over a surprisingly scenic slough. The next mile of the path traverses a marshy forest with star-flowered solomonseal and other woodland wildflowers. Then keep left along the shore past an old Forest Service guard station complex. Turn back at a canoe landing where the High Lakes Trail leaves the lakeshore for good.

Once you have returned to Aspen Point's fee booth, cross the road and continue 200 feet on the High Lakes Trail to a fork. To the right the Sunset Trail heads back to your car. If you're still not ready to call it quits, keep left to stay on the High Lakes Trail another 0.8 mile to an X-shaped trail junction beside Great Meadow. First detour left 50 feet to a viewpoint of the square-mile plain, which floods each April and May during snowmelt, attracting thousands of frogs — and the herons who eat them.

Then return 50 feet to the X-junction and go straight on the Family Loop Trail. This path ambles through the woods 0.7 mile and crosses a road to the Sunset Trail, where you turn left for 1.1 mile to return to your car.

Crater Lake's Rim Drive.

Index

A
Alice in Wonderland Trail, 42-43
Alta Lake, 118-119
Anderson Butte, 52-53
Annie Creek, 96-97
Applegate Lake, 66-67
Applegate Trails Association, 55
Ashland, 6, 18-19, 40-41
Aspen Point Campground, 130-131

Union Creek Resort.

B
Bandersnatch Trail, 42-43
Bears, 20, 27
Big Tree, 72-73
Bigelow Lakes, 74-75
Bigfoot trap, 66-67
Bloomsbury Books, 19

Blossom Bar, 83
Blue Lake Basin, 120-121
Boccard Point, 37
Boundary Trail, 70
Brown Mountain, 117, 126, 128-129
Brushy Bar, 82, 83

C
Cascade-Siskiyou National Monument, 34-39
Castle Crest wildflower loop, 9, 98-99
Cathedral Hills Park, 61-62
Chateau, The, 15
Clay Hill Lodge, 83
Cleetwood Cove Trail, 10, 106-108
Cliff Lake, 118-119
Cold Springs Trailhead, 124
Collings Mountain, 66-67
Cook and Green Pass, 68-69
Cougars, 20, 27
Crater Lake boat tours, 11, 106-107
Crater Lake Lodge, 8-9, 100-101
Crater Lake National Park, 7-12
Crater Lake Rim Drive, 10
Crater Lake Trolley, 7
Crater Peak, 112-113

D
Da-Ku-Be-Te-De Trail, 67

132

Darlingtonia, 76, 77
Deer Creek nature center, 77
Deming Gulch Trailhead, 57
Devils Backbone, 104-105
Devils Peak, 118-119
Diamond Lake, 13, 85-86
Difficulty levels, 25
Discovery Point, 102-103
Dogs, 26
Dollar Mountain, 61-62
E
East Applegate Ridge, 54-55
Echo Lake, 69
Eight Dollar Mountain, 76-77
Enchanted Forest, 63
Equipment, 27-28
F
Fees, 26
Fish Lake, 126-127
G
Garfield Peak, 100-101
Godfrey Glen, 96-97
GPS devices, 28
Grants Pass, 17, 60-62
Grants Pass Nature Trails, 61-62
Grass Lake, 118-119
Grave Creek Trailhead, 80
Grayback Mountain, 70-71
Great Meadow, 130-131
Grizzly Peak, 34-35
Grouse Gap, 46-47
H
Hart-Tish Park, 66-67
Heavenly Twin Lakes, 124-125

Coneflower has no petals.

Hobart Bluff, 36-37
Horn Bend, 78-79
Horseshoe Lake, 120-121
I
Illahe, 83
Illinois River Beaches, 78-79
Inspiration Point, 82-83
Isherwood Lake, 124-125

Island Lake, 120-121
J
Jack-Ash Trail, 52-53
Jacksonville, 17-18, 29, 58-59

Lake of the Woods Lodge.

K
Kerby Flat, 78-79
L
Lady of the Woods Loop, 98-99
Ladybug Gulch Trailhead, 64-65
Lake of the Woods, 116, 130-131
Lightning Spring, 102-103
Lilypad Lake, 69
Limpy Creek Trail, 61-62
Lithia Park, 19, 40-41
Little Illinois River Falls, 77
Little Pilot Peak, 37
Lower Table Rock, 29, 30-31
M
Madrone trees, 57, 60
Maps, topographic, 26
Margurette Lake, 117
Marial, 81, 82-83
Mazama Village, 96
McDonald Peak, 49
Medford, 29
Mike Uhtoff Trail, 44-45
Mosquitoes, 27
Mount Ashland Meadows, 46-47
Mount Bailey, 86
Mount Elijah, 74-75
Mount McLoughlin, 116, 122-123, 129
Mount Scott, 108-109
Mount Shasta, 39, 49
Mount Thielsen, 84, 87-88
Mule Creek Canyon, 16, 82-83
N
National Creek Falls, 89

133

Natural Bridge, 92-93
Nature Conservancy, 30
Northwest Forest Pass, 26
Northwest Nature Shop, 19

O
O'Brien Creek Trailhead, 70
Oredson-Todd Trailhead, 45
Oregon Caves Chateau, 15
Oregon Caves National Monument, 5, 14-15, 72-73, 74-75
Oregon Shakespeare Festival, 19
Oregon Vortex, 17

P
Pacific Crest Trail, 28
Paradise Lodge, 83
Park Headquarters, 9, 98-99
Parking fees, 26

William L. Sullivan.

Phantom Ship, 12, 106-108
Pilot Rock, 38-39
Pinnacles, The, 12, 110-111
Plaikni Falls, 11, 110-111
Prescott Park, 32-33

R
Rainie Falls, 16, 80-81
Rattlesnakes, 27
Red Buttes, 68-69
Red Queen Trail, 42-43
Rhyolite Ridge, 38-39
Rim Village, 100, 102
Rogue Gorge, 92-93

Rogue River, rafting, 16
Rogue River Trail (Lower), 5, 16, 80-83
Rogue River Trail (Upper), 92-95
Roxy Ann Peak, 32-33

S
Sasquatch, 66-67
Seven Lakes Basin, 118-119
Shakespearean Festival, 19
Silent Creek, 86
Siletz Tribe, 30
Siskiyou Field Institute, 77
Siskiyou Upland Trails Association, 52, 57
Sky Lakes Basin, 117, 124-125
Snailback Beach, 78-79
Soda Mountain, 1, 36-37
Split Rock, 48-49
Star Flat, 78-79
Star Ranger Station, 65
Steel Information Center, 9, 98
Sterling Ditch Tunnel, 56-57
Sun Notch, 112-113
Suspension footbridge, 79

T
Table Rocks, 30-31
Takelma Gorge, 94-95
Takelma Indians, 30, 82
Tallowbox Mountain, 64-65
The Chateau, 15
The Nature Conservancy, 30
The Pinnacles, 12, 110-111
The Watchman, 10, 104-105
Trapper Lake, 117, 125
Tunnel Ridge Trailhead, 56-57
Tututni Indians, 82

U
Uhtoff Trail, 44-45
Union Creek, 13, 90-91
Union Peak, 114-115
Upper Table Rock, 30-31

W
Wagner Butte, 50-51
Wagner Glade Gap, 49, 51
Watchman, The, 10, 104-105
Waters Creek Trail, 61-62
Whisky Creek cabin, 80-81
White Rabbit Trail, 44-45
Wilderness restrictions, 26
Wildflower identification, 21-24
Wildlife identification, 20
Wolf Creek Inn, 19
Wolves, 20, 27
Woodruff Bridge Picnic Area, 94

Made in the USA
Columbia, SC
09 April 2025